Muslim Calligraphy

Muslim Calligraphy

WITH 163 ILLUSTRATIONS OF ITS VARIOUS STYLES AND ORNAMENTAL DESIGNS

By
M. ZIAUDDIN
Lecturer in Islamic Studies, VISVA-BHARTI,
SANTINIKETAN,

KITAB BHAVAN
New Delhi-110002 (India)

Muslim Calligraphy

KITAB BHAVAN
Publishers, Distributors, Exporters & Importers
1784, Kalan Mahal, Darya Ganj,
New Delhi - 1100 02 (India)

Phones	:	(91-11) 23277392/93, 23274686, 32906494
Fax	:	(91-11) 23263383
Website	:	www.nusratalinasri.com
	:	www.kitabbhavan.com
Email	:	nasri@vsnl.com
	:	nusrat@bol.net.in

1st Indian Edition	:	1936
3rd Reprinted	:	2011
ISBN	:	81-7151-238-0
Book Code No.	:	M00130

Printed & Published in India by :
Nusrat Ali Nasri for **KITAB BHAVAN**
1784, Kalan Mahal, Darya Ganj,
New Delhi - 1100 02 [India]

DEDICATED

TO

SJ. NANDALAL BOSE

to whose sympathy and insight I
owe much of my appreciation of Mulim Art.

FOREWORD

I owe a word of explanation to the readers for the somewhat rambling arrangement of the matter presented in these pages. What appear as chapters in this booklet are only republished articles from the pages of the *Visva-Bharati Quarterly*, to which I was invited to contribute on the subject. When I first agreed to write, I did not realize the exact nature of the task that I had thus undertaken. For, as I proceeded with my work, I was amazed to find that this the most important aspect of Moslem art had not so far been treated with the comprehensiveness which a subject of its importance legitimately required. I found, for instance, that the influence of the Syriac and the Manæchian calligraphy on the early development of Moslem calligraphy had not received the attention that it deserved ; inscriptions, both monumental and decorative, had generally been considered from epigraphical point of view and rarely from that of calligraphy ; no serious attempt seemed to have been made to view the whole field of Moslem calligraphy as a unit in itself, with a clear historical background of its own, against which styles appeared and disappeared as they gave birth to newer styles and mannerisms, and which left their stamp on the decorative art of the Moslems ; it also appeared to me that a detailed and comparative study of the main features of the various styles, an analysis of their orthographical peculiarities was needed without which no scientific study of the subject could be complete.

I found myself therefore in the uncomfortable position of having to decide between writing a whole treatise on the subject, covering all its sides, or merely emphasising the points to which sufficient justice had not been done by previous writers on the subject, while at the same time giving the readers of the *Visva-Bharati Quarterly* a general idea of the character and history of Moslem calligraphy. The nature of my engagement, however, left me only the second alternative and I had to be content with the lack of compactness and proportion which may strike the reader as he reads these pages, and of which I am only too aware.

But even in this present form as the articles appeared in the *Quarterly*, they were received with so much appreciation by some kind readers, qualified to pronounce on the subject, that I was encouraged to publish these as a separate booklet in their original order.

I should be ungrateful if I did not acknowledge the debt that I owe to the numerous scholars who by their researches had made the field of work comparatively so easy to traverse, and but for whose collections of original specimens and photographs I should have been unable to illustrate the subject as profusely as I have done. I have quoted them wherever necessary.

M. ZIAUDDIN

Santiniketan.
7 September, 1936.

My pen works miracles, and rightly enough is the *form* of my words proud of its superiority over its *meaning*. To each of the curves of my letters the heavenly vault confesses its bondage in slavery, and the value of each of my strokes is eternity itself

MIR 'ALI.

TABLE OF CONTENTS

LIST OF PLATES

MOSLEM CALLIGRAPHY

INTRODUCTION.

Of all the arts that Moslems cultivated, calligraphy is, without doubt, the most refined. Writing as a decorative art was never practised by any people with such conscientious devotion as the Arabs gave it; nor did this art ever develop such an amazing variety of styles and expressions as it did among the people of Persia. These peoples valued written words more dearly than they did precious stones. To them the art of penmanship was superior to all other arts. Such was the lure of the line that from the monarch down to the humblest of writers, each vied with the other in writing beautifully. A calligraphist of repute was the artist whom people loved and honoured most and kings felt proud of possessing in their kingdom.

Moslems, so eager to avoid the painting and modelling of human figures, (there was no injunction of the Prophet to that effect, as it is commonly supposed), lest they relapse into their old ways of worshipping idols, the terror of which crime had been driven deep into their hearts by the thundering warnings of the Koran, devoted all their love and artistic ingenuity to the pious work of copying the Holy Word. A few of these copies that have survived from the early centuries of the Moslem era, are in themselves such idols of perfect rhythm and beauty that they leave the beholder inarticulate with admiration.

Islam, like some other great religions, appeared in the world as a magic force of Art. It gave a mighty impetus to the creative faculties of those who came under its sway. It welded tribes into a nation and set the imagination of men aflame. Important centres of culture like Mekka, Medina, Kufa, Damascus, Baghdad and Basra, etc., sprang up and worked like luminous melting pots where the remnants of ancient cultures were brought together and made to cohere into a brighter unity. The culture that later came to be distinguished as Islamic was the product of this fusion, and the language of art that was developed contained in it all the essential elements of pre-Islamic classical cultures.

Of the arts that were thus developed, the most remarkable became the decorative arts, amongst which the one that received its most characteristic development at the hands of the Moslems was the art of calligraphy. It was begun and carried on in its early stages by the Arabs, but received its highest fulfilment at the hands of the Persians. The book, with its beautifully written pages and finished cover, acquired such significance in the imagination of the artists that even architecture was stamped with its character and the wall surfaces were often finished as book covers.

The Arabs had a system of writing in pre-Islamic days. It had two styles: monumental and cursive. The cursive system was known to the Beduin poet, (at any rate by sight, since the Beduins were illiterate people), to whom it did not appeal as beautiful, for he has compared the scenes of death and desolation to words scribbled on parchment. " . . . the traces of a dwelling place which I saw and which filled me with sorrow," sang Imru'ul-Qais, "resembled the handwriting of a book upon South Arabian palm-bast."[1] Another poet says: "I came from Ziyad like one who is bereft of reason, my legs tracing different characters, writing on the road a *lām-alif*."[2] This quick and cursive style of the old Arabic script, used on soft material, like leather, palm-bast, parchment, papyrus, etc., must have existed prior to the monumental script. This latter and more developed script, used on harder material, like camel bones, especially ribs and shoulder blades, potsherds, flat white stones, wood and metals, became a great improvement in artistic effect. The Arab sense of geometrical symmetry and mathematical precision is well displayed in the execution of inscriptions wrought in this character. This style, as for example in the inscriptions of Yemen, has been admired as one of the most beautiful specimens of the writings of antiquity. As this style was used uniformly throughout Arabia proper, it must have been in use from very remote times.

From the point of view of adaptability to artistic use, unless I am biased, the Arabic script is by far the best we know of. It supplies vertical or oblique strokes and lines inclinable to any degree of angle, which, when merely repeated, would produce a linear rhythm delightful to the eye. This flexibility of line and stroke put at the disposal of the calligraphist, squares, circles, ovals, cubes, and loops, entwining and interlacing shafts, manageable to almost an infinite variety of quaint proportion and graceful curvature. During the Abba-

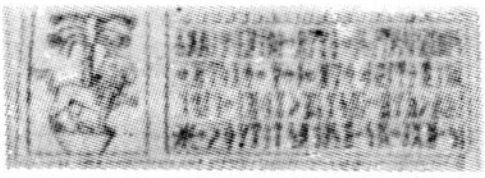

Fig. 1.
Early Himyaritic script on a bronze tablet in bas relief.

1. *'Ajab Nāmah,* A Volume of Oriental Studies, 1922, pp. 264, 265.
2. Ibid.

side period, the golden age of Islamic civilization, an immense number of styles of writing had developed which are extinct now. It was in that age that all the possibilities of the artistic utility of the Arabic script were explored. The variability of the Arabic script and its extreme sensitiveness to artistic suggestion is indeed amazing. All the letters possess a final flourish which may be turned in any becoming curve or angle, to any suitable length, to any proportion, in harmony or in contrast with the vertical shafts standing upright at their sides, marking time, as it were, to the flow of the music of composition.

Copying the Koran was deemed an extremely meritorious act. Aurangzeb, they say, lived on the money he earned by copying the holy Text Arthur Upham Pope observes : "The Koran was the sole way to life and salvation. Upon it depended the whole structure of society, the order of the day and the path to the future. Supernatural in origin, the final authority and standard of the good in life, it was deserving of every tribute that human skill could lavish upon it, and from the tenth to the twelfth century its pages were ornamented with such knowledge and such sure feeling for splendid design that these early pages remain today almost the greatest achievement in the history of Abstract art."[1]

The Moslems received the tradition of calligraphic art from the ancients. In Arabia itself, as I have already mentioned, a decorative style had been in use in pre-Islamic period. The Jews and the Christians had been copying their sacred literature with love and devotion. However, Islamic calligraphy owes its development more to the impetus that it received from the Manichaeans than to any other source. Although the Syrians were the first to initiate the Moslems into the art of moulding words into graceful forms, it was the Manichaean tradition that spurred it on to artistic heights.

The followers of the artist-prophet Mani were still very much devoted to the practice of calligraphying their scriptures when the Arabs conquered Persia. Their religion was particularly bound up with art. Whereas all the other messengers of God had received only a verbal revelation from their Lord, Mani alone had been vouchsafed divine paintings in illus-

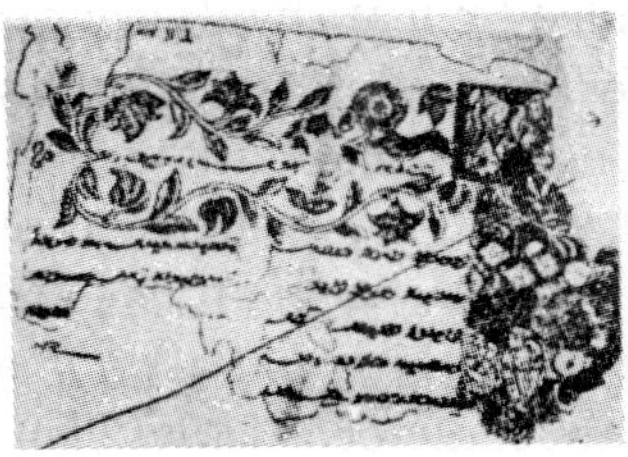

Fig. 2.
Fragment of a Manichaean page.

1. An Introduction to the Persian Art, 1930, p. 102.

tration of the stories revealed to him. He alone was endowed with prophecy as well as the miracle of art. When the ruling religion of Persia—Zoroastrianism—decided to save humanity from the menace of this new cult of light and shade, the revealed book was thrown into the fire before the eyes of the prophet. They say that rivulets of gold gushed out of the leaves as the flames licked them to ashes. In spite of successive persecutions, the followers of Mani continued to exist and they copied their literature with gorgeous illuminations. Till today the decorative splendour of the Book of Mani and the skill of his pen in tracing divine beauty are proverbial in Persia. Mani had invented a new script by blending the Syriac with Estrangelo. His works were written in this artistic script (Fig. 2.).

Moslems knew the Manichaeans by the name of Zindiq. They were famous for spending lavishly on the reproductions of their works. An Arab author has reported an interesting controversy in which Ibrahim Sindi says sarcastically : "I should be pleased if the Zindiq were to spend less on the whitest, finest paper and the blackest ink and on the training of calligraphists, for, indeed, I do not know of more beautiful paper than that of their books, nor of finer writings than one sees in their books. . . ." To this the other replies: "When the Zindiqs lavish so much wealth on the decoration of their books it is like the spending of the Christians on their churches. . . ."[1] Such works must have existed down to the fifth century of the Moslem era. Dr. Stein discovered a Manichaean manuscript at Turfan, in Central Asia, regarding which Professor A. von Le Coq writes that it is "written in the clear unequivocal letters of the Manichaean alphabet . . . beautiful and clear."[2] What we must particularly note is that this writing contains the punctuation mark, "the characteristic sign hitherto exclusively observed in Manichaean, namely, one or two black dots surrounded by little circles or ovals executed in red lead or vermilion."[3] In the earliest copies of the Koran a single verse of the Text was marked by a single circle ; a group of five verses was marked by a circle with a point at the top, usually in red.[4]

While the traditions and conventions of many peoples were at the back of the Moslem art, what was peculiarly Islamic in it was its lyrical character. In lyricism lay the individuality of the Moslem art.

---

1. Islamic Civilization, Khuda Bakhsh, Vol. I. p. 101.
2. Serindia, Vol. II. p. 819, plate, CLX II ; JRAS, 1911, p. 277.
3. Ibid., p. 278.
4. Encyclopaedia of Islam, vol. 1. p. 383, 384.

Pure Persian art of the Achaemenid and the Sasanid periods, as Mr. Roger Fry has observed, is devoid of lyrical element.[1] It seems, with the spread of Islam, a phase of romantic mood passed over Persia. What can be more lyrical than Persian poetry and the Nasta'liq calligraphy of the Moslem Persia ?

As I have mentioned, ornament is the speciality of the Moslem art, and, among their ornamental schemes, calligraphy has claimed their best attention. As in all other Moslem countries, so also in Egypt, "no art has been so much honoured or so assiduously cultivated," remarks Thomas Arnold, "as that of calligraphy. Whether in architecture or in the minor arts of domestic ornament, the highly decorative Arabic script was applied to all materials used, stone, plaster, wood, metal, ceramics, glass, textiles, etc."[2]

A line of calligraphic decoration, like a painting, stands in perfect harmony with its background. Its adaptability ensures its fitness with the surrounding scheme and gives it grace and life. On the other hand, its abstract nature calls for even greater artistic skill than is perhaps necessary in the case of painting pictures. In a painting, say of a beautiful lady, the artist can count on the co-operation of the beholder, who is familiar with the image in life and easily recognises in it life, grace and movement. In calligraphy the lines in themselves have to be so supple and round in form and graceful in movement that they must give the impression of being alive to the sight. Lines must move with grace and rhythm, while each of the curves and strokes keeps its balance in perfect poise. Thus rhythm, movement and grace have to be produced, not by reproducing the objects that possess them in actual life but by realising them in lines abstracted from those objects. Lines have to be sensitive and soulful, and, as it were, capable of muscular response to the slightest touch. In ancient Egyptian hieroglyphs, in which letters are mostly represented by natural objects, like hawk, vulture, duck, fly, man, etc., the beauty of the penmanship lies in the graceful outlines of the natural objects themselves. A mere glance at such a writing, for example the one inscribed on the ebony chair found in the tomb of Queen Hetep-Heres,[3] reveals the source of the artistic effect in the beautiful drawing of the objects which stand for letters. In the calligraphy of the Arabic script, however, the entire effect has to

---

1. The Exhibition of the Persian Art, Burlington House, 1931, Intr. p. XVIII.
2. The Art of Egypt, edited by Sir E. Denison Ross, 1931, p. 72.
3. Ibid. p. 116, fig. 2, Plate 4.

be achieved by the movement and poise of the lines, made, as it were, of the stuff of grace itself.

It has been observed that calligraphy has a subtle affinity with human and floral forms which gives it a remarkable adaptability to

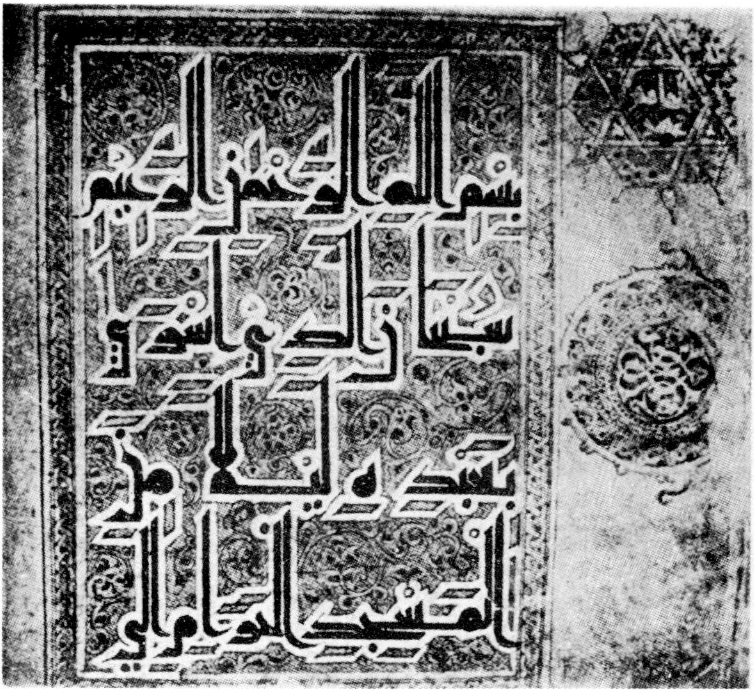

Fig. 3.

A Koran page in ornamental Kufic by Abu Bakr of Ghazna, 566 A.H.

pictorial rhythm. Mr. Roger Fry, comparing Chinese calligraphy with that of the Persians, remarks: "In this respect the fact that Chinese and Persian scripts are based on a much more free and flowing rhythm [than the Roman,] is of great importance since it enables the painter and decorative artists to combine calligraphy with pictorial forms in a single work of art. And in both countries alike we find this constant intermingling of script and painting. Perhaps in the matter of freedom and flow we must give the palm to the Arabic script, on account of its greater continuity. . . . And we find," he further observes, "both in miniature and pottery painting, the happiest and most unexpected effects produced by the incorporation of inscriptions in the pictorial or decorative designs. Even in their architecture . . . these inscriptions play a great part. . . . Nothing, I think, is more typical of the subtlety and ingenuity of the Persian genius than this peculiar interweaving of pictorial and literary elements through the special possibilities of the Arabic script. The practice seems to show how important a position system of *linear rhythm* held in the aesthetic sensibility of Persian artists."[1]

The calligraphist studies the flow of lines, their proportions and positions with a view to the rhythm he intends to impart to the given surface. The rhythmic harmony of strokes or curves of various patterns is studied with the mental vision of a composer of music (figs. 3, 4, 5.). Letters appear to the calligraphist as so many notes of music, and he sits to work out melodies out of them. A good painter is always a calligraphist. It is therefore not surprising, "that the lines with which the Persian painters outlined their human and animal figures express movement with an easy control and economy which is the envy of the Western artist."[2]

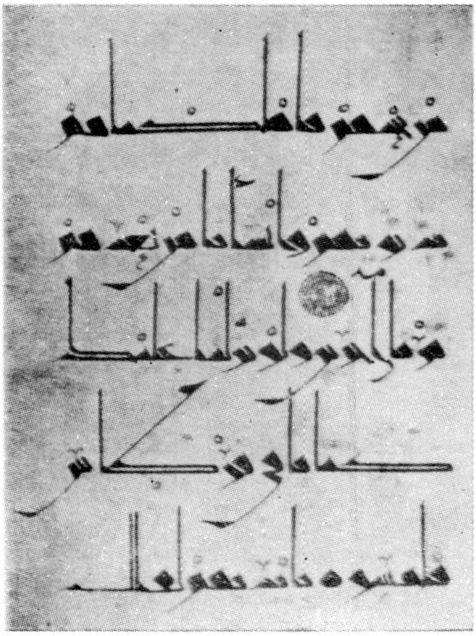

Fig. 4.
A Koran page in Kufic, 11th century, preserved in Toledo Museum of Art.

Among the ornamental designs that Europe borrowed from Moslems, calligraphic decoration was a conspicuous one. So great was the charm of the Arabic script as an ornament, that the Christian king Offa of Mercia (757-96) had his coin stamped with the Moslem religious formula in Kufic.[3] Another remarkable instance is the Irish bronze-gilt cross, of about the 9th century A.D., which has the word *bismillah* inscribed in the middle of it in Kufic. "In neither case," observes A. H. Christie, "can the workers have realized the significance of the strange writing they copied or adopted, for inscriptions so flagrantly

1. Persian Art, ed. by Sir E. Denison Ross, p. 34.
2. An Introduction to the Persian Art, p. XIX.
3. The Legacy of Islam, pp. 106, 113, 114.

Muhammadan could hardly have been set knowingly upon the coinage of a Christian king, or inserted on a sacred emblem."[1] In an Italian painting—the Resurrection of Lazarus, in the Arena Chapel at Padua—the right shoulder of the figure of Christ bears a lace, decorated with an imitation of Kufic. Fra Angelico and Fra Lippo had a particular weakness for the Arabic script and employed it even for sleeves of the Virgin and the borders of her robe.[2] Not only the decorative script, but other "ornamental details derived from Moslem sources became increasingly numerous in craft works wrought in Christian Europe."[3]

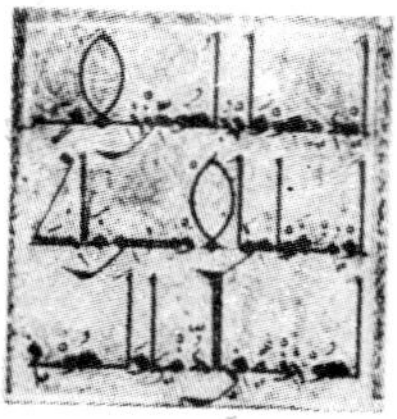

Fig. 5.

The art of Arab penmanship, like the other branches of their culture, reached its zenith of perfection in Spain. Their greatest achievement in architecture and architectural decorative art is seen in the palaces of Alhambra (figs. 6, 7). Even in ruins there is nothing in the world to be compared with them. "Its value for the history of art is incalculable. . . . Alhambra is unique." remarks J. Strzygowsky.[4] The delicate filigree work, the bewilderingly intricate tracery and the brilliant mosaic with superbly beautiful Kufic and other styles of calligraphic writings cut in relief, geometrically intricated bands in arabesques, which pleasantly confuse the observer with kaleidoscopic delusion, letters lengthening in intertwining shafts in profusion of beauty like water from a gay fountain, writings encircled by thickly clustering leaves waving on almost trembling twigs, reveal the standard of excellence that Spain had reached under the Moors. Pitchers placed in the niches of archs have beautiful verses written on them. One of them reads : "Incomparable is this basin ! Allah, the

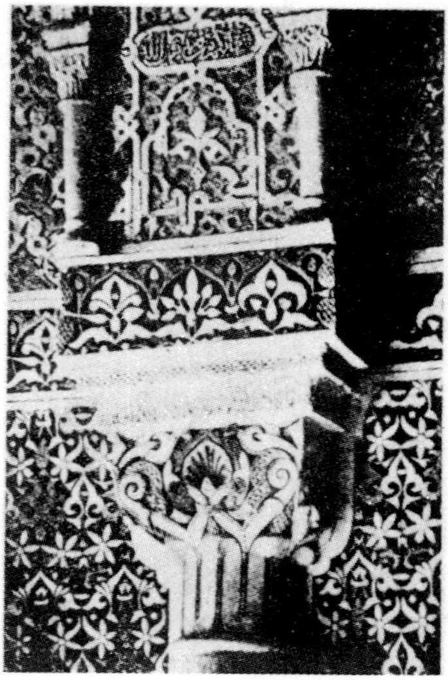

Fig. 6.
Alhambra. Capital and ornaments.

1. The Legacy of Islam, 1931, p. 114.
2. Ibid. p. 154.
3. Ibid, p. 114.
4. Encyclopaedia of Islam, vol. I. p. 278,

exalted one, desired that it should surpass every thing in wonderful beauty." Such pitchers placed in niches and inscribed with calligraphic writings are a speciality of the Alhambra. "None is powerful save God" is the phrase that one faces on all sides of the walls of the Alhambra.

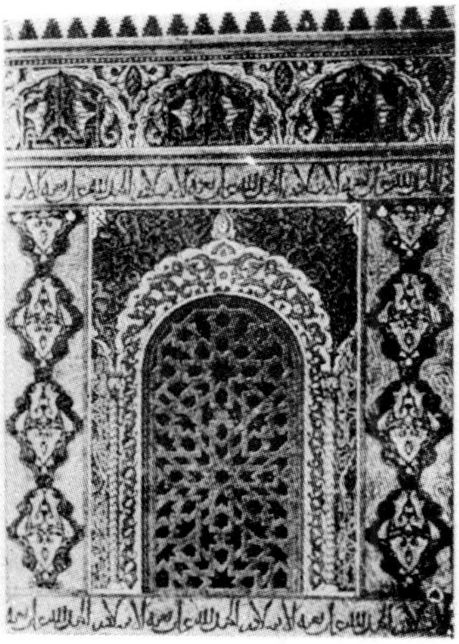

Fig. 7.
Alhambra, a window.

In Spain, as in Persia, blue and vermilion colours were most lavishly used in mosques and palaces. Very often the whole surface was coloured red or blue and then worked on in various hues. When the ground surface was red, the writing and other floral and linear designs were painted blue, black, green and yellow. The single tombstone left in Spain (Alhambra) is painted blue and the writing is done in gold. As in the main features of the decorative plans of architecture, the schemes of colour too appear to have been borrowed from the illuminations of books. Wall surfaces were divided into rectangular panels with raised margins, and either completely covered with intricate stucco work or glazed tiles, or with brilliant mosaic faience. The whole surface from top to bottom was ablaze with the grandeur of colours. The deep blue or red was the favourite ground colour; golden yellow, white, black, emerald green and turquoise lined the decorations. The Kufic or Naskhi in white or gold on deepest blue gave an effect which can not be described in so many words. Referring to the glazed ceramics and their decorative motifs, Dr. Pope writes: "Arabesque and stellate medallions, stately personages or gay, galloping cavaliers, lordly Kufic, or Kufic as delicate as stuccato cadenzas, rendered in gold and cobalt, green, turquoise, maroon and black, were all woven into the loveliest of compositions. Theme and material, colour and pattern are as unified and as gracious as a sonnet."[1]

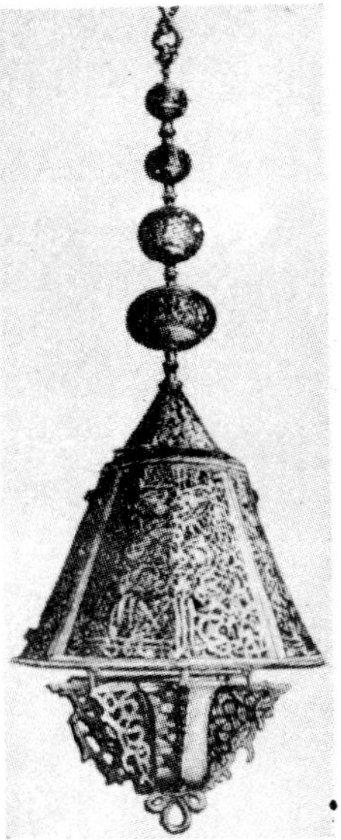

Fig. 8.
A mosque lamp (Granada).

1. Studio, Jan. 1931. p. 14.

Arabs had developed a very high standard in the craft of leather tanning and that of making parchments. To Kufa belongs the credit of discovering methods of tanning leather. After tanning the leather or parchment membrane, they dyed it in silver or gold and polished it to such a degree that it reflected the face of the observer like a mirror. The writing was executed in vermilion, green, black or blue. The ink they made has not yet been successfully imitated in Europe. Book covers were lavishly decorated with gold and silver and sometimes inlaid with jewels.

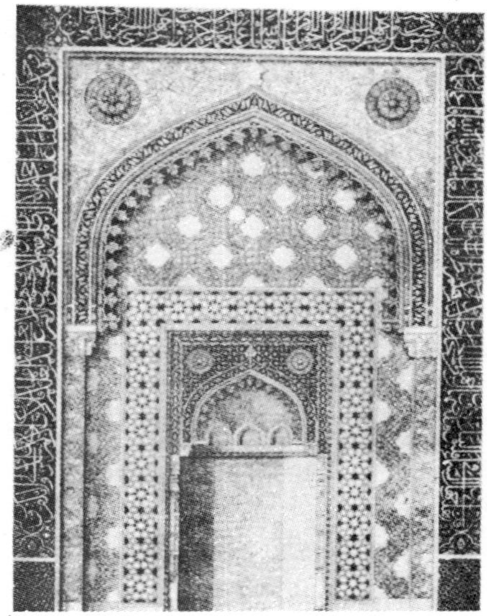

Fig. 9.

Mihrab of the Jami' mosque at Fatehpur Sikri, 1556-1605 A. D.; the architrave is painted deep blue, sculptured with verses from the Koran in Naskh, overlaid in gold.

The Arabic script, both in its simple and intricated ornamental forms, charmed the eye like magic. It was imitated as arabesque and supplied pure calligraphic motifs in the decoration of churches and shrines in Italy, Spain and France. And thus, quite unknowingly, as Mr. S. P. Scott remarks in his *History of the Moorish Empire in Europe* (Vol. III, ch. 29.), verses of the Koran were quoted on church walls in Kufic. He remarks, quoting a French author, that the lofty gate of the most important church of St. Peter was decorated with the Moslem confession of faith in Arabic script. Obviously, the script must have in it something of the universal appeal to the artistic nature of man, for, otherwise, Christians would not have allowed this Arabic script to enter their sanctuaries. In spite of such a catholic appreciation that calligraphy inspired, Mr. E. Herzfeld makes the strange remark : "It is undoubtedly an expression of a certain bigotry on the part of the Muslims, that they inscribe nearly every article of artistic craftsmanship with some verse from the

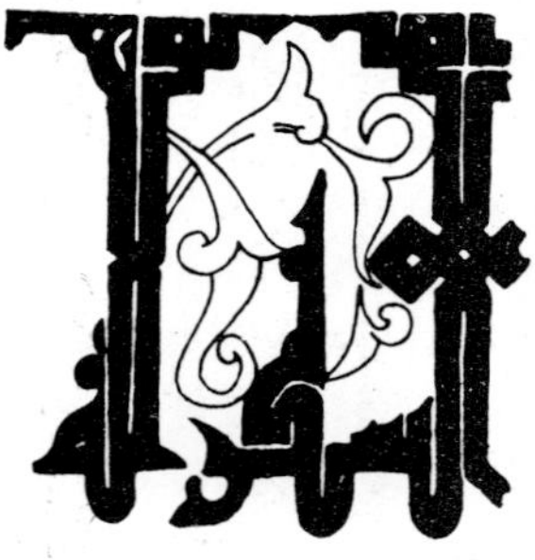

Fig. 10.

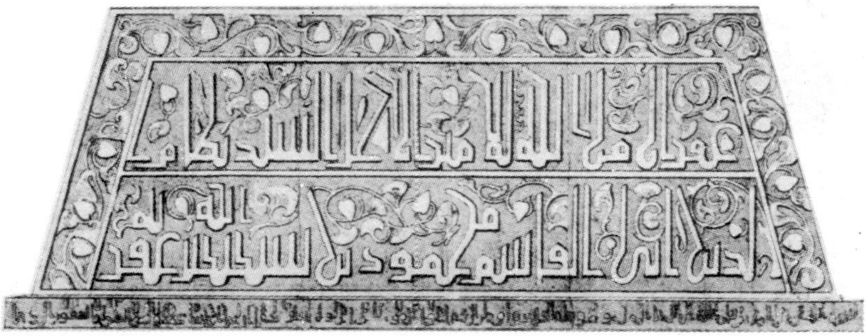

Fig. 11.
The inscription in floriated Kufic on the tomb of Mahmud of Ghazna.

Koran. . . ."[1] Out of such inscriptions, he is ready to accept certain inscriptions "with gratitude because of their historical importance."[2] Otherwise such writings appear to him "rather a peculiarly decorative use of the characters . . . " which are "the confession of faith or with innumerable, sometimes rather pointless, formulas of blessing or congratulations. . . ."[3] The formula of the confession of the Moslem faith, which in a few letters contains the whole of Islam, is, naturally, very important to a Moslem. This confession, when abbreviated to its initial letters is summed up in letters, L. A. M. (the three letters with which the Koran begins are A. L. M.)

Fig 12.
Kufic inscription in plaster relief, with an undercurrent of spiral stalks—on the mihrab of the Mosque of Yahya bin Abul Qasim, 543/1148, at Mosul. The name of the calligraphist is signed as Mustapha Baghdadi.

These three letters have been used as architectural motifs of decoration with incomparable ingenuity of designs. As symbol of faith few Moslems would be able to recognize their confession of faith in these three letters, but men of all faiths would undoubtedly find them beautiful. Mr. E. Herzfeld admits, however, that the decorative value of these letters lies in "their rhythmical and symmetrical shape."[4] Furthermore, ignoring the calligraphic value of such decorations, he

1. Encyclopaedia of Islam, Vol. I, p. 364.
2. Ibid, p. 364.
3. Ibid, p. 365.
4. Ibid, p. 365.

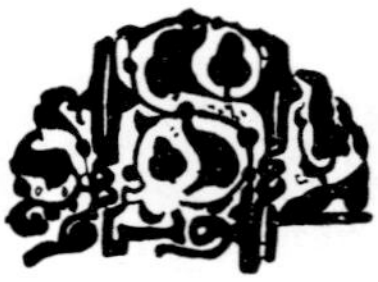

Fig. 13.

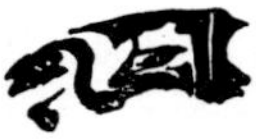

Fig. 14.

Fig. 15.

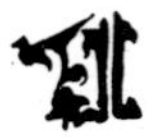

Fig. 16.

Floriated Kufic decorations from lustred plates.

observes with regret that these letters, "the nature of which has been completely misunderstood, are found on objects made by non-Moslem artisans especially on Western imitation of Arab works of art."[1] Later on this decorative writing "developed into a particular kind of linear ornament," he remarks, "in which all consciousness of the original nature of the letters was lost."[2] This was bound to take place. The peculiarity of the Arab mind lies in its tendency to abstract the qualities of Nature and give them an independent form. They abstracted the linear rhythm of their calligraphy and applied the new rhythmical elements thus gained to their arabesque.

After the extermination of the Moors from Spain, Moslem masons were sought to build churches and shrines. They were not paid for their labour, but, in return, were exempted from the poll tax. These Moslem builders must be to a great extent responsible for the style that Christian architecture developed and also for the introduction of the calligraphic motifs.[3] For it was actually after the fall of the Moslem rule in Spain that Christian architecture came into existence. "The Muhammadans," writes Mr. Owen Jones, "very early in their history, formed and perfected a style of art peculiarly their own. . . .

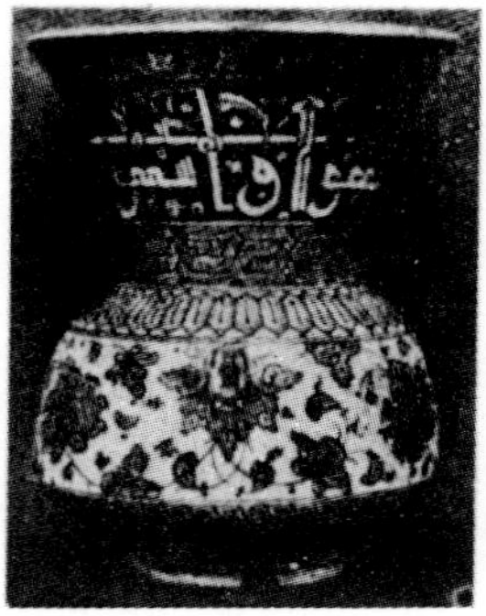

Fig. 17.
Anatolian lamp, XVI century.

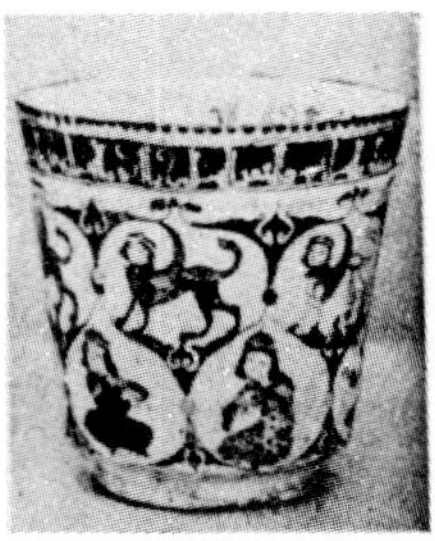

Fig. 18.
Cup with decorative Kufic, XII—XIII centuries, Ray.

1. Ibid, p. 365.
2. Ibid, p. 365.
3. The Legacy of Islam, p. 13.

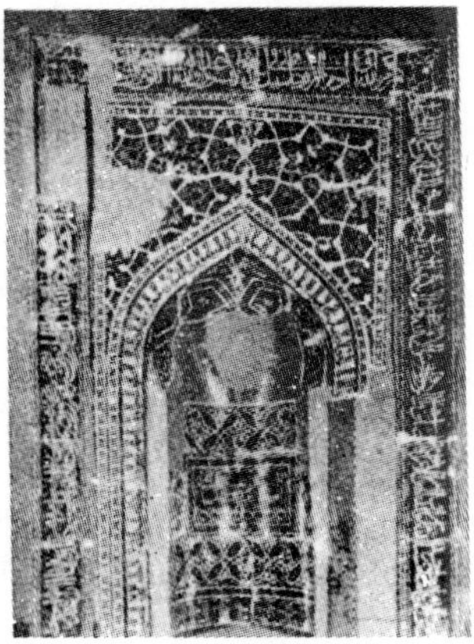

Fig. 19.
Mihrab, with Kufic and Naskhi inscriptions in mosaic faience, XIV century, Persia.

It can hardly be said that Christianity produced an architecture peculiarly its own, and entirely freed from traces of paganism, until the twelfth or thirteenth century."[1] "The carved inscriptions used decoratively in late Gothic work," writes Mr. M. S. Briggs, "were anticipated in the ninth century at Ibn Tulun's mosque at Cairo, but inscriptions in Kufic characters penetrated far into France during the Moslem occupation of her southern provinces, and rare examples of ornament even in England are believed to show Arabic influence." [2] Prof. Lethaby considers the bands of ornament on the retable of Westminster Abbey and also on certain stained-glass windows to be the result of the influence of Moslem calligraphy on English decorative art. [3]

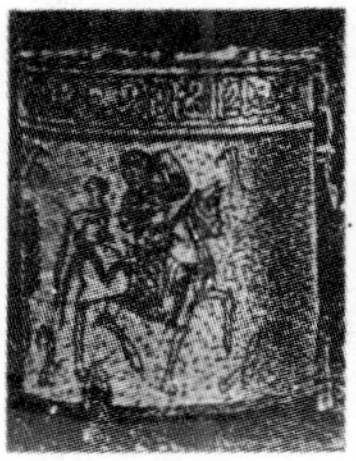

Fig. 20.
Painted ivory box XIII, century.

While we possess relics of Moslem arts of all the countries that are or were under Moslem rule, Spain alone has an almost blank page. Libraries, mosques, palaces, baths, and indeed all the main and minor products of art were destroyed by Christian barbarians of Spain with a thoroughness unparalleled in the history of humanity. As S. P. Scott has observed, the clergy declared Arabic script to be magic formulas and Arabic works to be books on magic ; laws were enforced to wipe off every sign of them from Spain. And thus we have lost what must have been of the greatest value to art.[4] Books were hunted up, piled up in crossways and set to fire. Ferdinand IV. and Charles V. started the scheme of destroying the remains of Moslem culture in

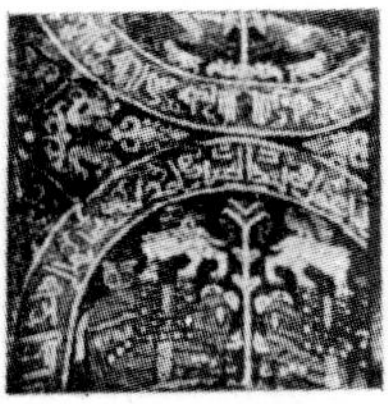

Fig. 21.
Baghdad silk, X—XI century, with Kufic writing in arch bands, woven in red, yellow, black and white.

1. The Grammar of Ornament, 1910, p. 57.
2. The Legacy of Islam, p. 178.
3. Ibid, p. 178, foot note.
4. History of the Moorish Empire in Europe, Vol. III, ch. 29th.

Spain.[1] Philip II. gave orders to the effect that every stone bearing Arabic writing should be broken to pieces. One may wonder how the silver-gilt-plated casket, adorned with pearls, belonging to the scholar

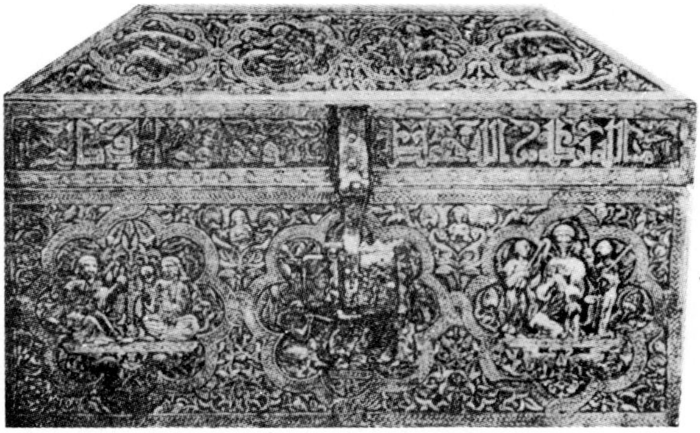

Fig. 22.
An ivory casket, XI century, with floriated Kufic on the border of the lid, in the cathedral of Pamplona.

king of Spain, Hakam II., and bearing a beautiful inscription in Kufic that invokes blessing on the owner, found its way on the high altar of the cathedral of Gerona.[2]

Calligraphy, like all fine arts, is beyond definition. We cannot bring out its points of beauty by analyzing it into its original components. Hence, particularly in the case of decorative calligraphy, it is difficult to understand or appreciate its complete artistic significance without referring the original to its proper setting and back-ground. Most of the illustrations used in this study are pieces of calligraphy cut off from their main body, bereft of their original colours and can therefore hardly give us any exact idea of their native artistic effect. In the next section I intend to deal with only one of the various styles of the Moslem calligraphic art, namely, the Kufic, and will try to present to the readers some of the most characteristic decorative variations of this style.[3] The merit and the ornamental charm of each variation of the main style can be appreciated by comparing it with the others. I must also mention that I have not considered it necessary to burden the study by giving the usual chronological list of the early calligraphists. About most of them nothing more than their name and the style they wrote in is known. Of their works nothing worth mentioning has come down to us. Moreover, as in architecture and

1. The Moors in Spain, S. Lane Poole, 5th ed. pp. 272, 273.
2. Ibid, p. 148.
3. The remaining styles will be dealt with in two more sections in the next number of this Journal.

painting, it is difficult to determine exactly the period of the development of Kufic styles, which, like other styles of later periods, appear and disappear with the rise and fall of dynasties. Styles have evolved into different styles so slowly and imperceptibly that we can only refer to their dates in terms of the centuries of the reigns of certain kings.

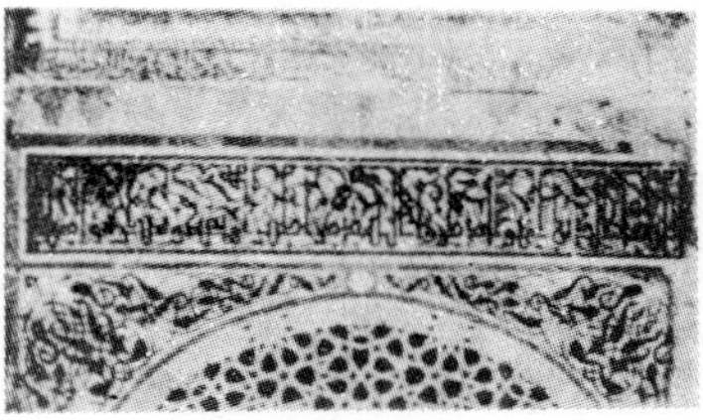

fig. 23.
Madrasat-ul-'Attarin (Fez), a panel with floriated Kufic in mosaic faience.

KUFIC

THE Kufic or the angular variety of the Arabic script, has been traced to about a hundred years before the foundation of the town Kufa (17/638), to which place the style owes its name. It was first in this town that this particular way of writing was officially made use of. This official recognition gave the style its present name. It was a hieratic script and was treated as such throughout the period it continued to be employed. For about the first five centuries the holy Koran was exclusively written in the various forms of this style (figs. 24, 25, 26, 27, 29).

For the first two centuries of the Moslem era, they were mostly the Arabs who cultivated the art of calligraphy. During this period calligraphy does not seem to have advanced beyond its strict use, that is, it did not evolve any purely decorative form. The Koran dated the 168 A. H. is in simple Kufic. The simple and unshakable faith of the early Moslems, which the bold and rhythmic oratory of the Koran had inspired in the proud and unbending Arab, did not consider the fickle and flowing style of writing used by the traders in towns to be at all a suitable medium for the holy Word to be couched in. The Kufic was just the script for it ; it suited in form the bold character of the revelation.

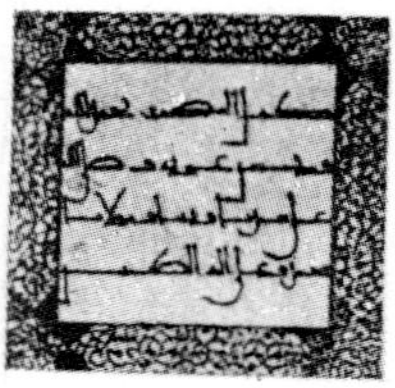

fig. 24.
Carpet with a verse from the Koran in cursive Kufic

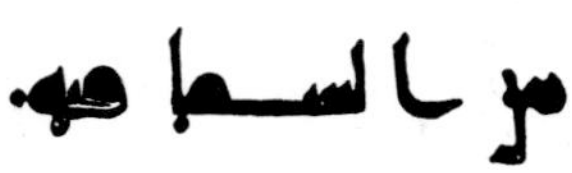

Fig. 25.

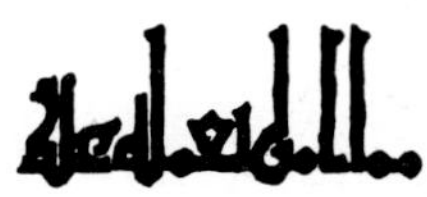

Fig. 26.

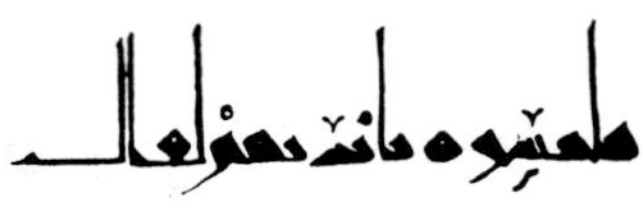

Fig. 27.

These earliest forms of the Arabic script, the cursive and the monumental, are immediately derived from the Nabataean, which itself is ultimately traceable to the Phoenician of the eighth century B. C. It was termed Himyaritic, Himyar being the town where it was current before the advent of Islam. Some of the inscriptions in this character are adorned with animal and tree figures, done in conventional styles. The Sabaean inscriptions have, in some instances, their last letter decorated with an ornamental design.[1]

The Himyaritic or Sabaean writing, owing to the hardness of the

1. Indian Antiquary, Jan. 1875, p. 28.

material it was written on, developed a blunt, straight and sharply angular character (fig. 28). The other more common system, due to the soft medium it was used on and also the necessity of writing quickly, developed a flowing and cursive form. This cursive style, as it further developed into the Arabic script, later called Naskhi, was in fact used on papyrus and parchment, before the angular Kufic came into existence. Historically, the Arabic script is the youngest the world has produced, but with regard to its use in the world today, it is second only to the Roman.

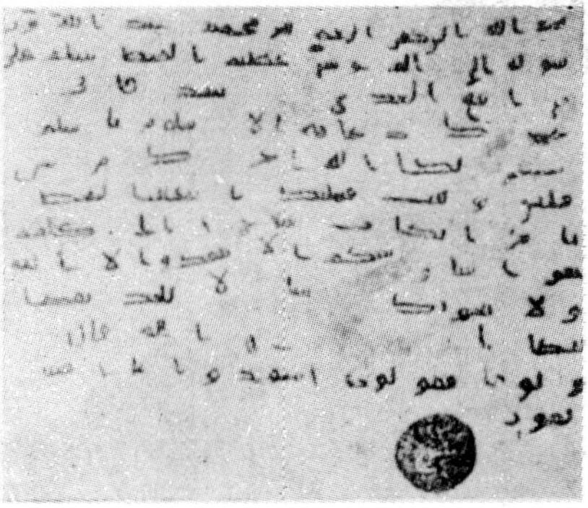

Fig. 28.
Letter of the Prophet to the "Mukaukas" written in the 7th year of the Hijra.

The cursive style, when written after the Syriac model of writing, to which script the Arabic one is very closely related, developed into regular Kufic (fig. 25). The main features of the Kufic mode of writing are its vertical and oblique lines. The earlier cursive style, as used in pre-Islamic days, had already developed the fundamental character of the Arabic script, namely, the ligatures that joined one letter to another. These connecting strokes were to prove of immense importance in their use as graceful ornamental flourishes. This script was, however, defective in short vowels, it had no diacritical dots to differentiate similar letters from each other. These marks it received during the 2nd century of the Moslem era.

Kufic writing seems to have reached its extreme angular character by the end of the 2nd century of the Hijra. Thenceforward the rounder script begins to curb it to softer curves. The 3rd century Koran has rounder curves and slantingly pointed tips (fig. 33). By the middle of the 4th century the Kufic gives way to the Naskhi, that is, to a little rounder script, and, more or less, ceases to be employed in the copying of the Koran, though continues to be used as ornament. The Fatimid dynasty of Egypt (550/1155) made the most of the Kufic style, and practically with the passing of this dynasty, the script also fell out of use and became obsolete, except in architectural and ceramic decorations. Its most fantastically ornamental forms, intertwining, interlacing, floral and geometrical, evolved during the 5th and the 6th centuries of the Hijra.

In the beginning, as already mentioned, it was the simple Syrian model of calligraphy that suggested to the Arabs further improvements in their script. Diacritical dots and signs were adopted after the Syriac model. This influence of the Syriac system of writing had actually begun before the advent of Islam. The vowel marks were also taken from the Syriac, but these were different from those in use now. They were indeed the Syrian Moslems, familiar with the Syriac and Hebrew scripts, who are known to have first improved the lettering of the Arabic script. They determined the form of each letter of the Arabic script in its simple and compound form and defined its vowel marks, after the standard of the Syriac.[1] This step must be considered the first definite move towards the development of the art of calligraphy. Different styles of Kufic developed gradually. Abul Aswad (69 A. H.), a disciple of the Kalif 'Ali, is reported to have improved the calligraphy of the Koran and introduced vowel marks in the form of dots. His system was followed for about a century. His disciples improved upon his style. Qutba is the next great calligraphist who is said to have invented four styles of the Kufic. After him we hear of Khalid (96/715), who stood out foremost amongst the artists of his period. The golden inscription on the Prophet's Mosque is believed to be the work of his penmanship. He also copied the first Koran we hear to have been illuminated with gold. In the Abbaside period, with the rise of monarchy and the growth of wealth and knowledge, the profession of the calligraphist received all the encouragement that an art might need. Mekka, Medina, Basra, Kufa and Baghdad, etc., had their own schools of art.

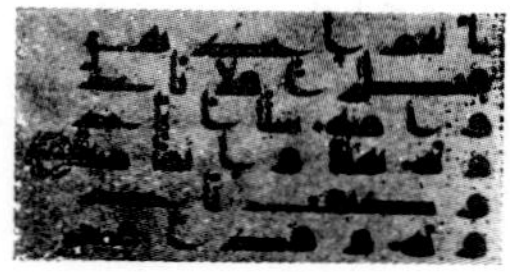

Fig. 29.
A page from the Kufic Koran on deer skin, II century of the Hijra.

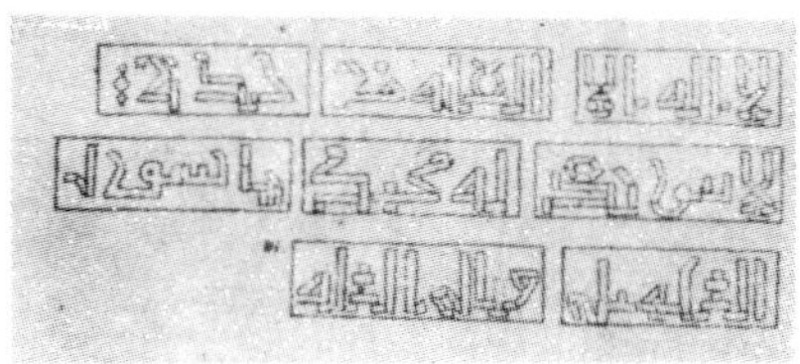

Fig. 30.

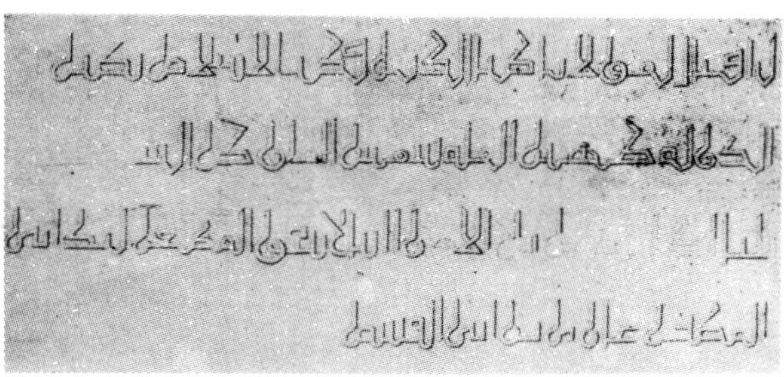

Fig. 31.

1. Subhu l-A'sha, Vol. III, pp. 12-14.

Another age in the development of the Kufic calligraphy sets in with Khalil bin Ahmad (170 A. H.), the grammarian, and Ali bin Kusai (182 A. H.). Improvements introduced by them have been, more or less, retained to the present day. Kusai was the teacher of Mamun ar-Rashid. And Mamun ar-Rashid was the first lover of the art of calligraphy who collected as many specimens of good penmanship of all the various styles as could be obtained in his kingdom.

The Persians in pre-Islamic age are reported to have invented seven different styles of writing their language. All these styles differed according to the nature of the subject matter they contained or the person they were addressed to. Moslems seem to have classified some of their styles according to this old custom of the Persians. Most of these styles were combinations of one or more styles of the Kufic. For example, there was Al-Jali, the bold Kufic, used in royal correspondence and monumental inscriptions. The Sijjalat was the documental Kufic. Salasi was used in letters addressed to officials and subordinates. Miftah was a style compounded of the Salasin style and the Estrangelo script. Haram was the style used in letters addressed to ladies, etc. Styles used in the calligraphy of the Koran were other than these. The Kufic reached its excellence in the calligraphist Ibn Muqla (338 A. H.), who was a renowned artist of the reign of Al-Qahir-Billah the Abbaside. He is said to have invented the five main styles that prevailed after the Kufic lost its charm for the people.

The letter, believed to be the very epistle of the Prophet that he wrote to the "Mukaukas" written in the 7th year of the Hijra (fig. 28), is perhaps the earliest specimen of the Arabic writing of the Moslem period. It differs from the cursive only in its stiffness and angularity. It presents the very form of the Arabic system of writing that calligraphers set to improve and beautify a few years later. A definite improvement is observable in the monuments of the period immediately following that of the Prophet. The mile-stone (fig. 32), marking 109 miles from Damascus, belonging to the reign of the Kalif Abdul Malik bin Marwan (65-86 A. H.), shows the marked improvement that calligraphy had gained over the previous style. Notwithstanding

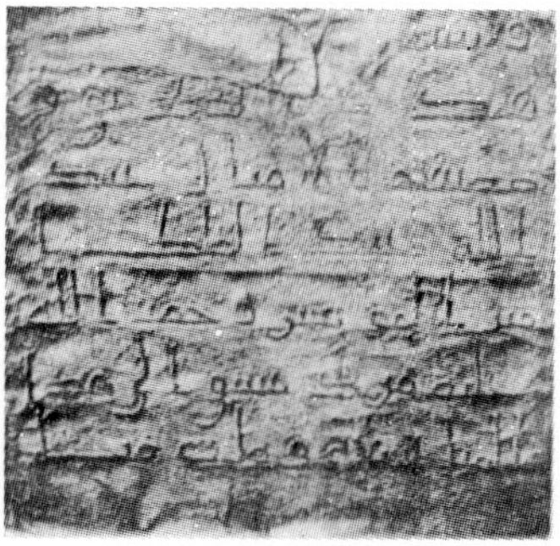

Fig. 32.

the ravages of time that this mile-stone has withstood during the last fourteen centuries, it has kept much of its beauty intact. Letters are no longer irregular and wayward, they stand in order and keep their proportion and symmetry of form. The whole composition gives beautiful calligraphic effect. Compared to the letter of the Prophet the writing of this stone is less angular and less stiff.

Another Kufic inscription (fig. 33), engraved on marble and dated 155/771 A. D., belonging to the Mosque Al-Mahdi, is an example of the regular Kufic that had developed during the 1st and the 2nd centuries of the Moslem era, before the ornamental Kufic came into existence. The tips of the strokes, both vertical and oblique, are pointed, and, sometimes, have a flourish added to the vertical shafts. The whole composition is compact and the lettering precise ; no vowel-dots are used in any of these two inscriptions.

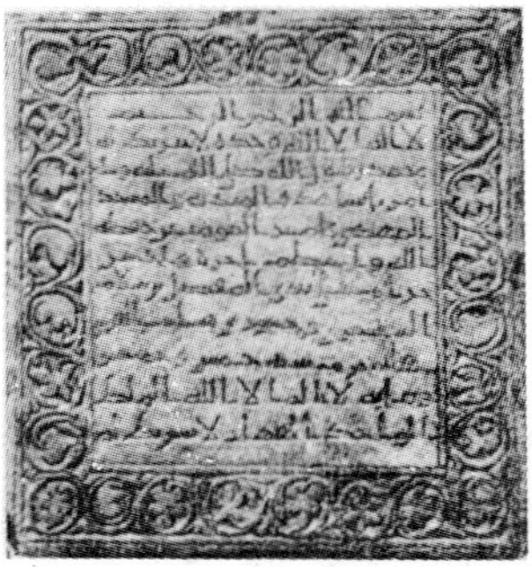

Fig. 33.

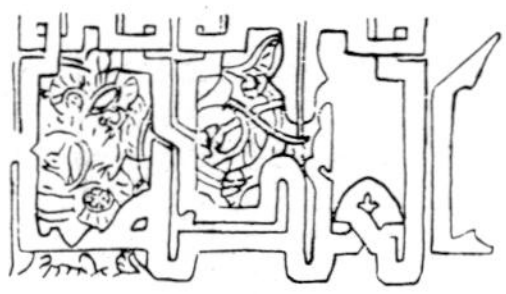

Fig. 34.

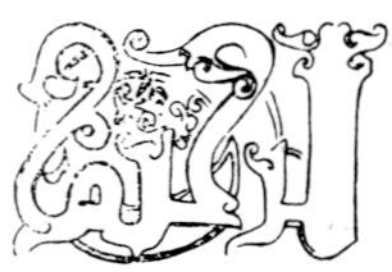

Fig. 35.

Fragments of the Kufic writing on the niche of a mosque at Mosul, dated 576 A. H.

By the first quarter of the 2nd century of the Hijra, the Arabs had their rule established beyond the western shore of the Caspian sea in the Russian territory. Some of the Kufic inscriptions discovered in Darband and Baku, by M. N. de Khanikoff, are in striking contrast to the regular style of the Kufic writings of that period.[1] The calligraphists there, in many instances, have definitely declined to follow the angular Kufic of Baghdad that prevailed in the then Moslem world. Their ideal was the cursive style of the papyrus. However, when this comparatively rounder style is cut in stone, it keeps neither the character of the angular Kufic nor that of the cursive. It develops an independent style which is somewhere between the two.

1. Journal Asiatique, 1862, p. 103.

The fac-simile of the inscription given by M. N. de Khanikoff, dated 175 or 195 A. H., is in the Kufic of the ultra round style.[1] It also bears the vowel dots. The lettering of this inscription is extremely beautiful. I am inclined to believe that the calligraphy of those inscriptions must have been deeply influenced by the then prevalent Syriac. The Syriac inscription, d. 677 A. D., discovered in the cemetery of Khusrav,[2] Persia (fig. 37), will bear witness to the intimate resemblance that exists between the Baku inscriptions and this Syriac writing. The letters in it are traced in their outlines, which method was also followed, sometimes in the copying of the Koran. The vowel dots that were adopted in the Arabic system from the Syriac are observable in this specimen in their original form. In the early Kufic too, as in this Syriac inscription, words ran horizontally, for which peculiarity the style was named *maqur*, i. e. walking on all fours, in the manner of the quadrupeds (compare figs. 37, 38, 39).

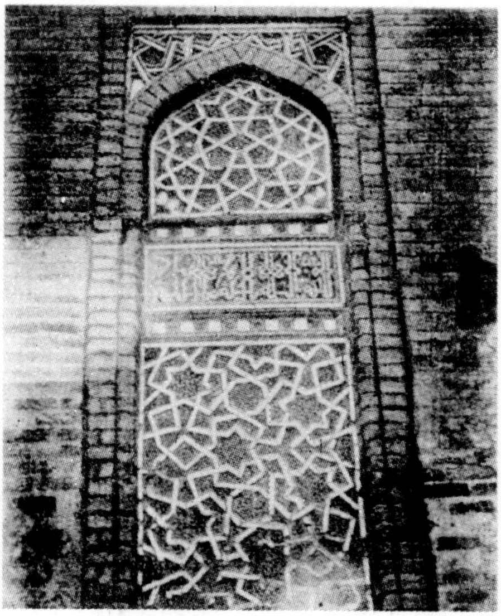

Fig. 36.
Plaited Kufic in relief on a pretence door in the Mosque of Abul Qasim, at Mosul (543/1148).

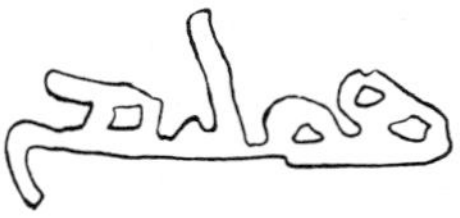

Fig. 37.

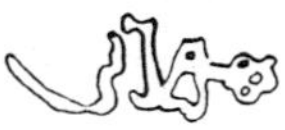

Fig. 38.

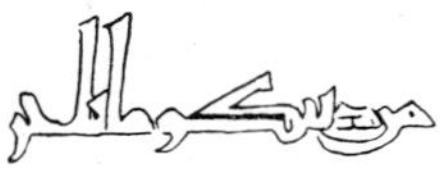

Fig. 39.

The principle which separates one style of the Kufic from the other of the class, is the principle of different proportions in which vertical lines stand to the oblique ones and the intervening curves, and also the proportion that the breadth of the line has to its length ; the unit of measure being the square dot that the pen makes with its point, without being pressed beyond its actual breadth. For instance, the long connecting

1. Journal Asiatique, 1862, p. 103.
2. Journal Asiatique, Jan. 1885, p. 44.

links of letters that give an oblong character to the style may be shortened and the words rendered square in form. The word Muhammad, which in Kufic has generally an oblong position, may be pressed into square dimensions by shortening the length of the connecting links of its letters (fig. 40).

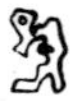

40.

I have already remarked that the Caucasus styles of Kufic are peculiar in themselves. As an example of this peculiarity I may refer to the Baku inscription dated 471 A. H. on the mosque built by Ar-Rashid b. Muhammad b. Abi Bakr (fig. 41). The first glance at it is sure to convince us of its originality. It cannot be classed among the styles of the Kufic that are known to have existed in different parts of the Moslem world. Its letters are simple and undecorated. The distinctivē feature of it lies in the irregular treatment of its vertical strokes, which are short, flat at the top or pointed and stand out like a row of irregular teeth; the oblique strokes, along with the main horizontal bases of the words are distorted so that the composition of the inscription has lost one half of the essential character of the Kufic style. The word *al-Masjid* (fig. 42) is bent in a semi-circular position. The basic lines are either tilted or given a long undulating curve.

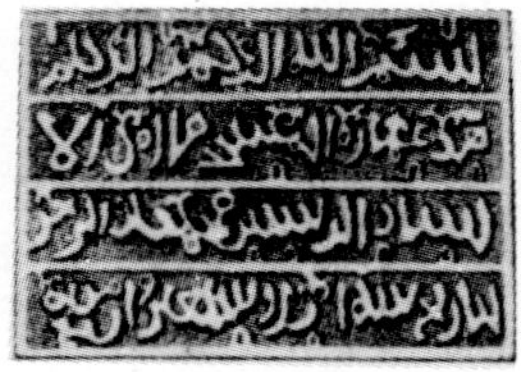

Fig. 41.

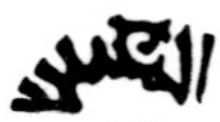

Fig. 42.

The inscription dated 557 A. H., engraved on the sanctuary of Yusaf b. Kabir (fig. 43) presents another peculiarity of the Caucasian Kufic. The novelty of the style is distinctly observable in the treatment that each word of the composition receives individually. The word Zaki, at the end of the first line, is written in a zigzag form. The four vertical shafts of the word (a)l-Isla(m) are joined with two horizontal lines above so that we have two triangles placed over the word as sheltering roofs.

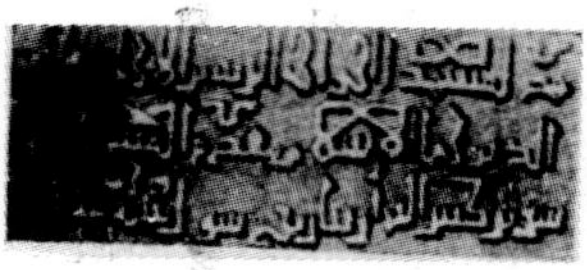

Fig. 43.

It would appear that the people of the Caucasus mountains, being more or less cut off from the cultured provinces in the south, continued to play with the first model of the Kufic that entered their country earlier than it did any other. Though it almost ceased to be used in other countries by the end of the 5th century of the Hijra,

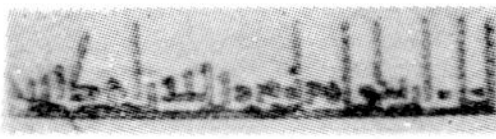

Fig. 44.

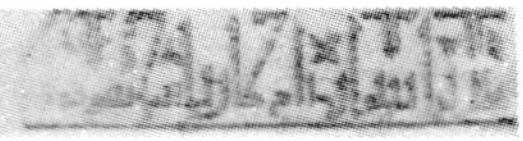

Fig. 45.

the Caucasian calligraphist used it down to the 8th. They indeed took it more as an ornament than as the script of a language. What is more amazing is that they seem to have worked their inscriptions as individual pieces of artistic work, not necessarily connected with other inscriptions in the mode of their lettering (figs. 44, 45). The tombstone dated 670 A. H. gives us a unique style of a fantastic writing, in which the round variety of the Kufic is treated in a manner that the writing gives the impression more of a work wrought by the corrosive forces of Nature on cemented floor than of the chisel of the artist. The features of the letters are concealed by breaking the continuity of their lines and by giving them fantastic, and, as though unintentionally, most unexpected dimensions, resembling the unmindful scribbling of a child that has just learnt to write his ABC. The result is extravagant to the point of being bizarre. The word *sa'd*, if I have rightly followed Dr. Khanikoff's reading of this inscription, shows the letter *d* (at the left end of the word), in its peculiar flourish.

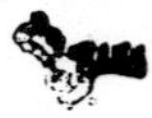

Fig. 46.

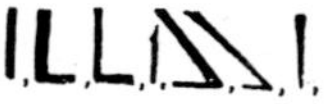

47.

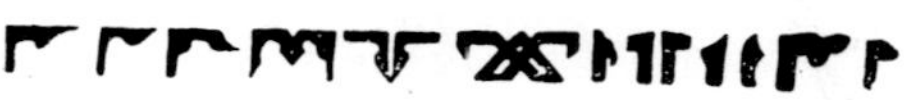

48.

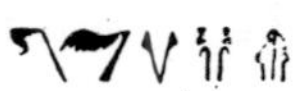

49.

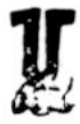

50.

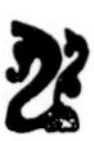

51.

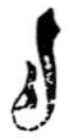

52.

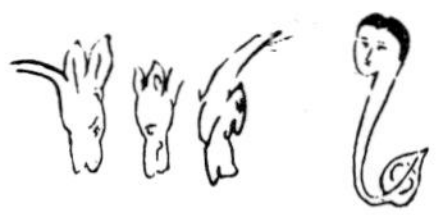

53.

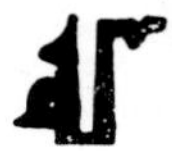

54.

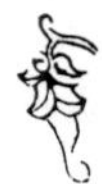

55.

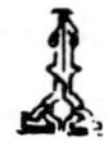

56.

A vertical line, standing by itself or occurring at the end of a word, represents the letter *a* of the Arabic alphabet and forms part of many other letters. There is no end to the manner in which this vertical stroke may be written. It may have a flat top, a pointed one ; the point may be slanting to the right or to the left, may have a small line projected to either of its sides, or both sides in the shape of an arrow ; it may taper upwards or downwards, the line itself may bend to any moderately acute angle or curve ; it may curve at the top in the shape of a hook ; bend one way and coil to the other in any graceful manner (figs. 47, 48, 49, 50, 51, 52).

If the writing is executed in extreme angular style the letters take the form of rectangular or square blocks piled one on the other to compose words (fig. 30).

Vertical strokes, when they occur in succession as in the word Allah, may be written in uniform height, or in gradually descending order, or the middle one shorter than the two of equal height on both the sides ; or the middle one may be taller than the either on each side (figs. 57, 58). All these shafts may also rise to equal heights, intertwine and interlace (figs. 7, 10, 59, 65), or bend against each other in oval curves (fig. 5).

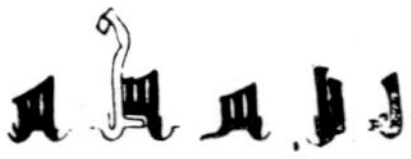

Fig. 57.

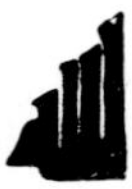

58.

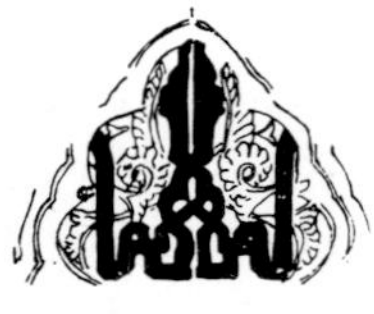

59.

The stroke may be suddenly bent at any point on its body once or more than once (fig. 60) and straightened again. These bends may be sharply angular or round. Instead of these bends the stroke might have a simple knot or two ; the knot may be interlaced. A stroke may be written in double lines in a variety of ways, interlacing (figs. 60,61,62,63) or entwining once or more than once. Strokes that lie apart from each other, the oblique ones or curves intervening them, may also be brought to interlace each other once or more than once.

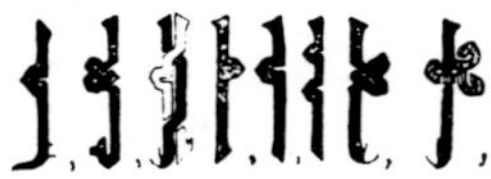

60.

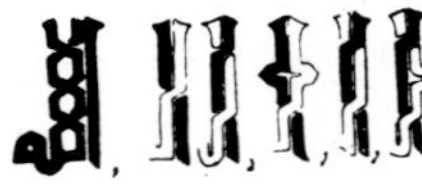

61.

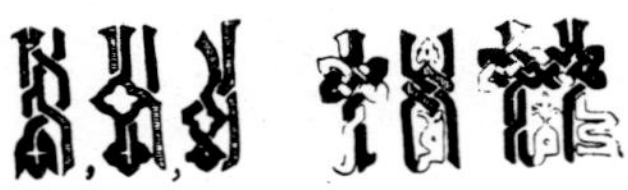

62.

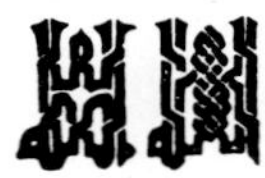

63.

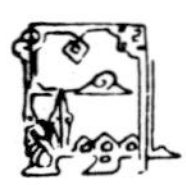

Vertical strokes may also be so joined together at the top that they form a horizontal rafter over the word, and may be woven into geometrical or floral figures. This arrangement divides words into compartments, and the triangles hanging from the horizontal bar above give the impression of chandaliers. Such compartments may be ornamented with wheeling twigs and swaying leaves with graceful sweeps from one compartment of the word to the other (figs. 10, 34, 23, 53, 65).

65.

The oblique line is also treated in the same way. It primarily

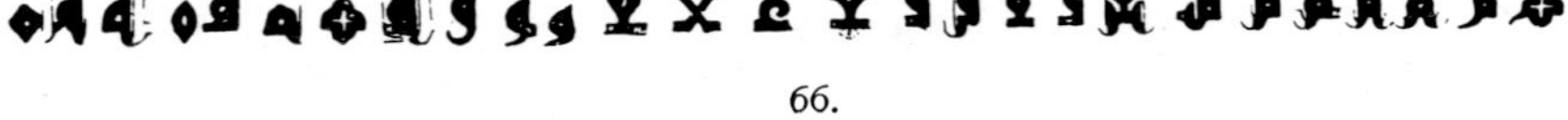

66.

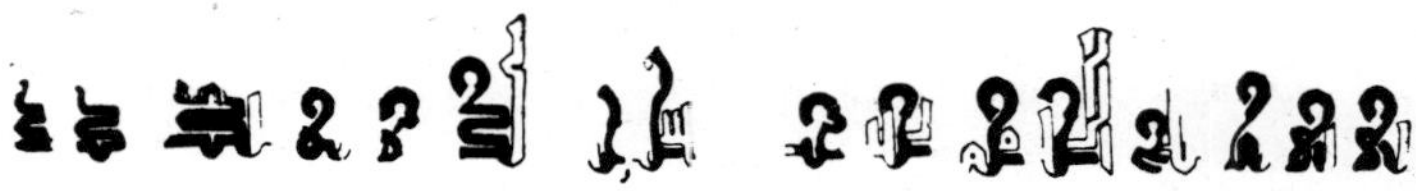

Fig. 67.

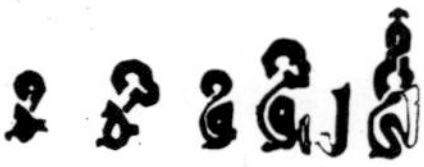

Fig. 68.

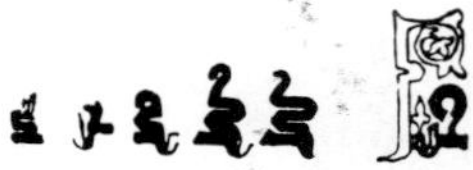

Fig. 69.

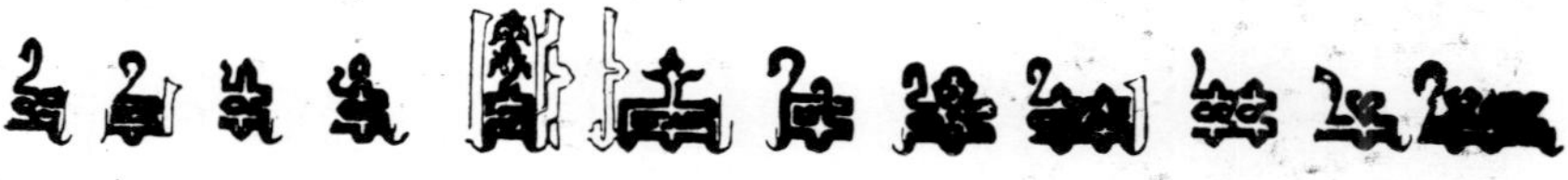

Fig. 70.

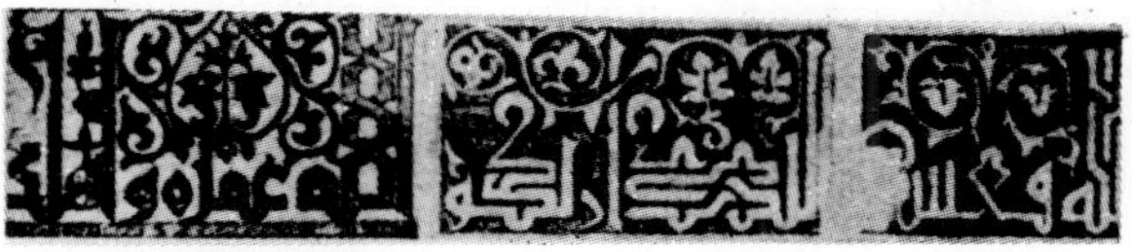

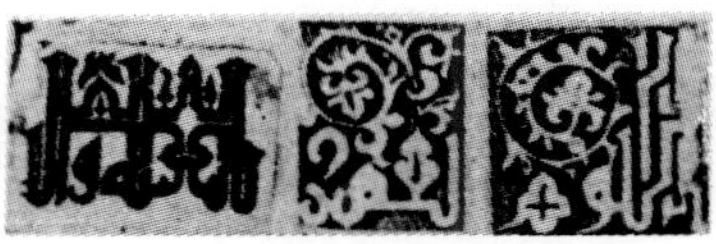

Fig. 71.

serves the purpose of joining two letters together and also forms part of some of the letters of the Arabic alphabet. It may be simply doubled, twisted once or more than once and, in case it forms a separate letter, may end in a leaf, a loop or any proportionate geometrical figure. These oblique shafts may also interlace or entwine in various ways as shown in figures above

The square, oval or circle also forms part of some letters. It may be written in any decorative form which does not completely change the character of the stroke, may also have extra flourishes and may be drawn in lines entwining each other.

Fig. 72.

Every kind of line, especially the vertical one, may broaden and blossom into any floral form or terminate in an animal or, though very rarely, in a human face (fig. 53), it may be executed in the form of a capital of a pillar with spiral corners(fig. 72).

The Chinese seal pattern proved such a success that often the lattice work of screen, cut in marble, wood or plaster was worked out in the Kufic in most ingenious manners. In this triangular Kufic vertical and oblique lines were woven into each other in fret-work (figs. 73, 74, 75).

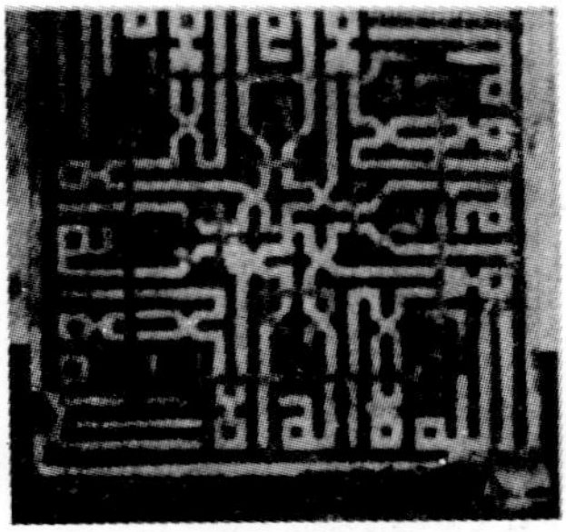

Fig. 73.

Though extremely beautiful, the Kufic style, during the first five centuries of the Moslem era, developed into an absolutely ornamental style and it became impossible to continue it as the script of the Koran. Its use became strictly ornamental and the common cursive style, quick, less angular and less decorative, was adopted for the Koran. This style which had been in use side by side with the Kufic was developed by calligraphists and termed the Naskh, the subject of our next section.[1]

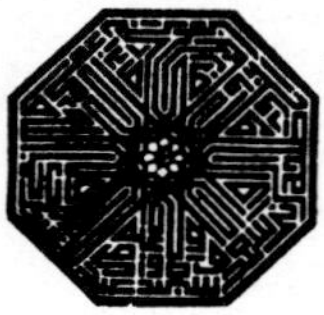

Fig. 74.

Fig. 75.

1. I have reproduced with gratitude some of the details given by Mr. S. Flury of the Kufic inscriptions of Kisimkazi Mosque (Zanzibar), in his article in JRAS, April, 1922.

II

THE POSITION OF A CALLIGRAPHIST

BEFORE we proceed to discuss the other styles of Calligraphy, it seems to me desirable that a few words should be said on the position of a calligraphist and his art in the Moslem Society.

In the days of the Abbasides, with the introduction of paper, [1] and the spread of culture among the masses, the institution of education and the art of book production gained supreme importance. What was then called *warāqat*, consisted of the profession of transcribing manuscripts, of book-binding, gilding and the business of selling books.[2] *Warāqat* flourished as an honourable pursuit for literary men and scholars of every description. The great demand for quick work in the copying of books had produced a class of prolific scribes who combined the merit of speed with that of a beautiful hand-writing and were specially called *warrāq*. The learned as well as the officers of the government employed them as secretaries and amanuenses.

In those days the publication of a book was an event of great social importance. It meant business to the calligraphist as a class, reputation to the author with a hope of immortality and enrichment of knowledge to students. An author either delivered his work as a lecture from the pulpit of a mosque, or read out from his notes with commentary in extempore, while scribes and students dispersed among the audience noted down his words with incredible speed. Dictation (*imlā*) ran for days, months, even years, according to the extent of the thesis.[3] Scribes then compared their texts with each other, and corrected their copies according to the one certified by the author as correct and reliable. These texts were then copied again and sold in the book-market. Authors wrote scores of volumes and it is difficult to believe today how they managed to write single handed such encyclopaedic works as they have produced.[4]

---

1. Fihrist, p. 32.
2. Ibid, p. 169. ; Ibn Khaldun, Cairo, I, pp. 349, 350, 351.
3. Ibn Khallikan, II, p. 228; Fihrist, p. 299.
4. Ibid., I, p. 297 ; Nafkhut-Tib, II, p. 884.

Authors had no rights of royalty over their works. Once broadcasted among students and scribes and through them to the world, the author lost every connection with his work. Any body could copy and sell it as his own property. There was a time when misappropriation of authorship was common. Authors, in order to save their authorship, took the precaution of mentioning their name in full in the text, as many times as they could manage. Poorer authors wrote their works, copied them and sold them at the door of their house or by auction in the streets of the town.[1]

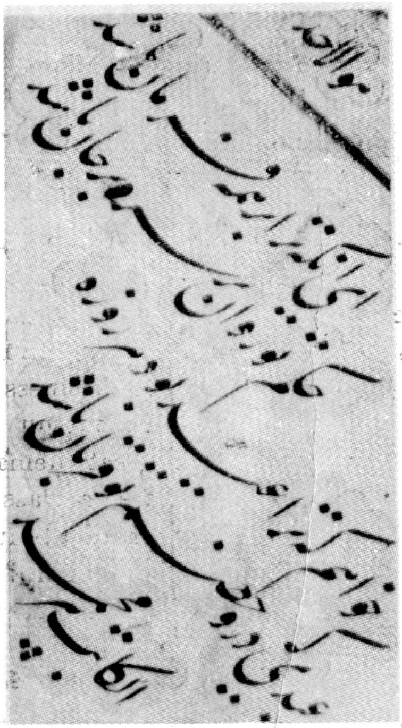

Fig. 76.
A panel of Nasta'liq calligraphy by Pir Muhammad (Kala-Bhavan Museum, Santiniketan).

Book-shops generally clustered round the principal mosque of the locality and formed the book-market. Baghdad had about three hundred bookshops. Bookshops were the principal resort of the learned. Book-sellers being generally scholars and authors of repute were the centres of attraction for all seekers of knowledge. Here in the midst of polished and gilded manusscripts squatted the respectable and the learned and discussed poetry and religion till midnight.

Speed in the transcription of a text was a matter of keen contest between scribes. The calligraphist of the court of the prince Bayasanghar is reported to have written three thousand lines of poetry in one day and night. During the time he was performing the feat, hundreds of people had gathered round the palace at Mashed, and drums were being beaten in full fury to stir up the excitement that the occasion had created.[2] Yahya bin Adi was such a fast hand that he could write one hundred pages in twenty-four hours.[3]

1. Ibn Khallikan, I, p. 63.
2. Tazkira-i-Khushnawisan, p. 47.
3. Tarikhul-Hukama, p. 369.

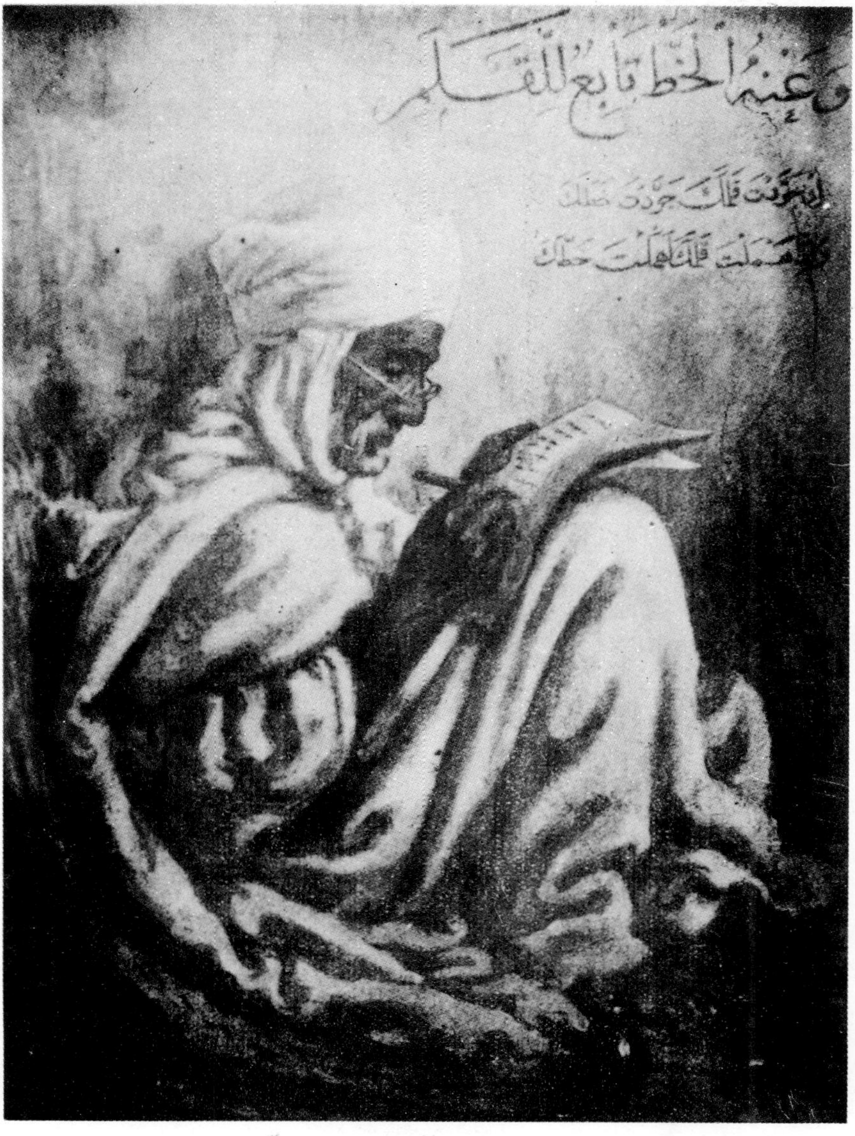

Fig. 77.

Portrait of a Moroccan calligraphist, by E. Dinet

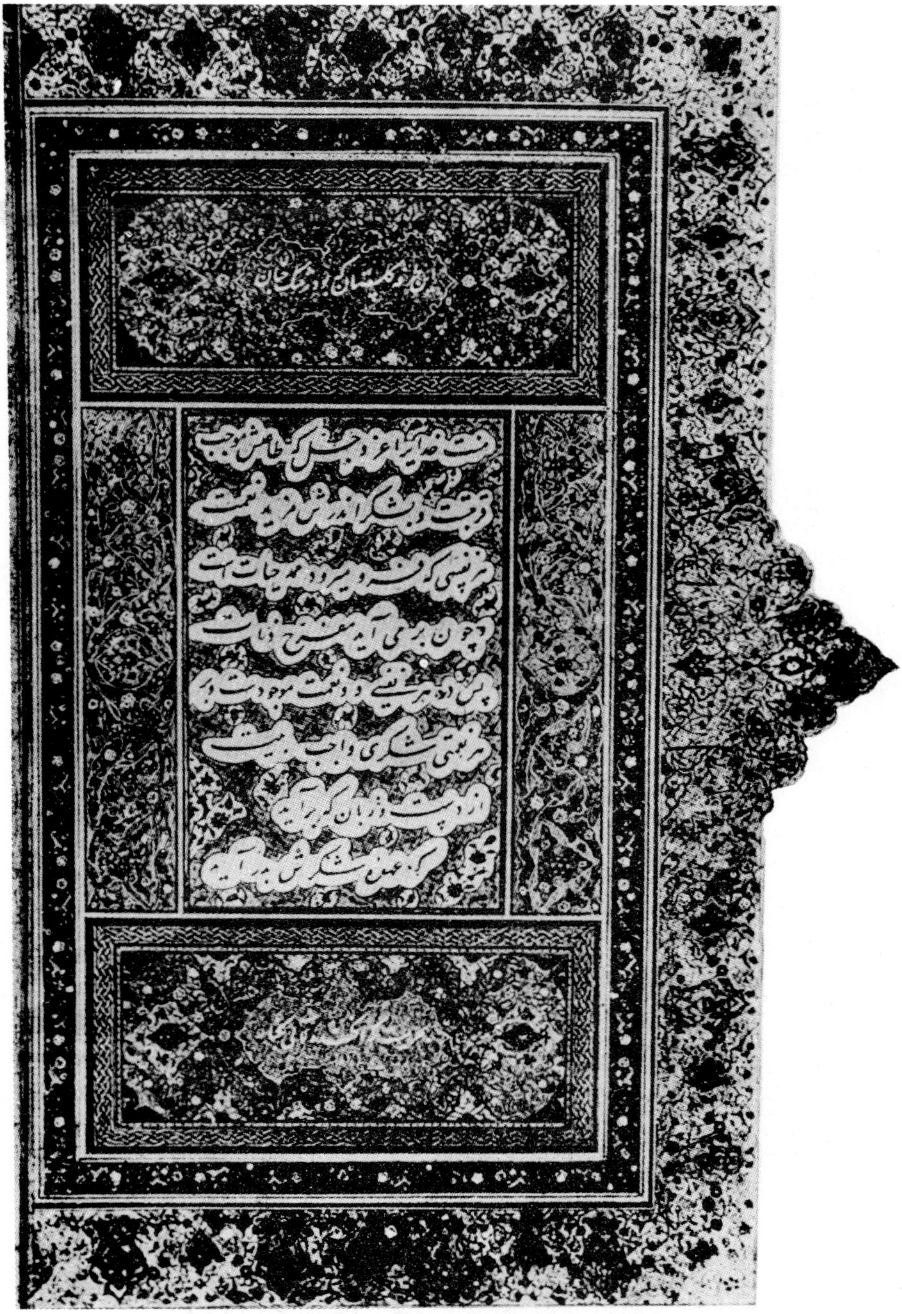

Fig. 78.

Front page of the *Gulistan* of Sa'di, calligraphed by Mir 'Ali for Shah 'Abdul 'Aziz Bahadur of Bukhara, in 950/1543 (Monuments et Mémoires, 1918—1919, p. 189, Pl. XV ; the fringes have been, unfortunately, omitted by the block-maker).

The profession of a copyist being fairly profitable, literary men and scholars adopted it. Normally, their daily income through copying saleable books was three to four rupees.[1] They were also employed in libraries for transcribing books and were paid regular remuneration. They were appointed as teachers, the most reputed among them being selected for instructing princes, princesses and sons of nobles. Often a prince had more than one teacher in calligraphy, each being in charge of the particular kind of hand he specialized in. Calligraphists were given charge of libraries where their duty was to supervise the work of subordinate scribes engaged in copying books and look to the quality of their handwriting. Remuneration of a scribe depended on the quality of his hand, the average of his mistakes and his speed. Mullah Muhammad Amin of Kashan, the superintendent of the library of 'Abdur Rahim Khan Khanan (who was a remarkable penman himself), was paid a monthly salary of four thousand rupees.[2] But the Khan Khanan's liberality was proverbial ; most of his artists enjoyed *jagirs* too. In the library of Banu 'Ammar, at Tripoli, one hundred and eighty scribes worked, of whom a group of thirty could always be seen at work day and night.[3] In the royal library of Bayasanghar, who was a calligraphist himself, forty scribes worked under the supervision of Maulana Ja'far.[4]

Scribes were very often scholars of recognised status and while they served as copyists they could do their own creative work too. For example, Ibn Sa'd was a copyist of Waqidi and has written a stupendous biography of the Prophet.[5]

Every nation, at the height of its culture, has given proofs of its love for knowledge by founding public schools and libraries, but with Moslems the desire had amounted almost to madness. Nothing satisfied their vanity so much as the number of books in their libraries. Books were often written at the request of Kalifs and nobles who paid huge amounts of money for their labour. Mansur the Andalusian had received five thousand coins of gold for his *Fusus*.[6] Part of a Kalif's palace was always a library. Princes, courtiers, nobles and the rich gloried with the scholars in possessing

1. Yaqut, III, pp. 85 ; refer also to p. 105.
2. Islamic Culture, Oct., 1931, p. 627.
3. Transactions of the 7th A. I. O. Conference, 1933, p. 1032.
4. Tazkira-i-Khushnawisan, p. 45.
5. Fihrist, p. 145.
6. Nafkhut-Tib, II, p. 728.

rare manuscripts in their libraries. The palace of a Kalif was a library as well as the debate house of the empire where men of talent of all religions and nationalities were brought together to solve religious and intellectual problems, with the king as their president.

Adjoining the halls of the library were studios where hundreds of calligraphists copied books, while painters illustrated them with miniatures, binders bound them in leather and gilders and illuminators finished them as pieces of artistic production. Scribes were often grouped into separate rooms according to subjects of their transcription. The calligraphists of the Koran were grouped together and so were the copyists of books on tradition, biography, history, law and medicine, etc. Some of them were appointed to go through the copied manuscripts and add short vowels and diacritical marks.[1]

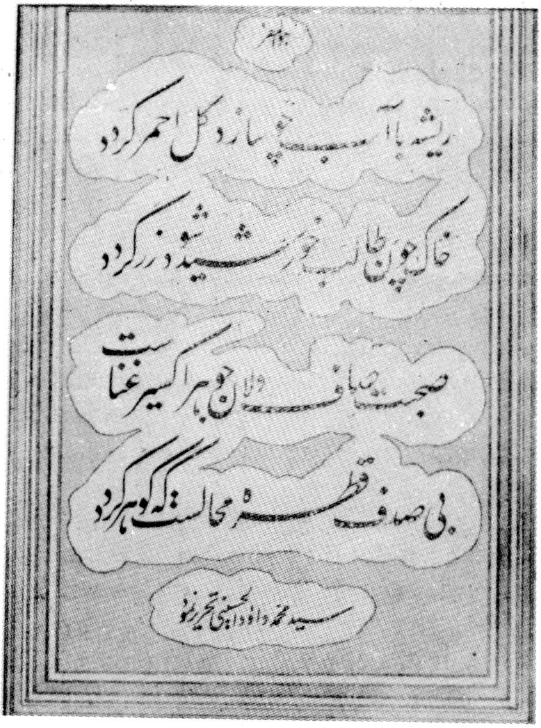

Fig. 79.
A beautiful and delicate specimen of Nasta'liq calligraphy by Sayyad Muhammad Da'udal-Husaini of Kabul.

Never was there so great a demand for beautifully written manuscripts as in those days of the Abbasides. The standard and the style set up by the Kalifs was followed by their subjects. And most of the profit accruing on the pious work of educating the masses and of collecting libraries for public or private use, went to the class of the calligraphists.

The amount of work the scribes had on hand in the Capital towns of the empire is not possible to guess. Yet an idea may

1. Ibn Khallikan II, p. 334 ; T. Atibba, II, p. 234—236 ; Almaqrizi Khitat, I., pp. 409, 458 ; Yaqut, V, p. 447 ; Ibn Khaldun, IV, p. 146 ; Ibn Khallikan, I, p. 144.

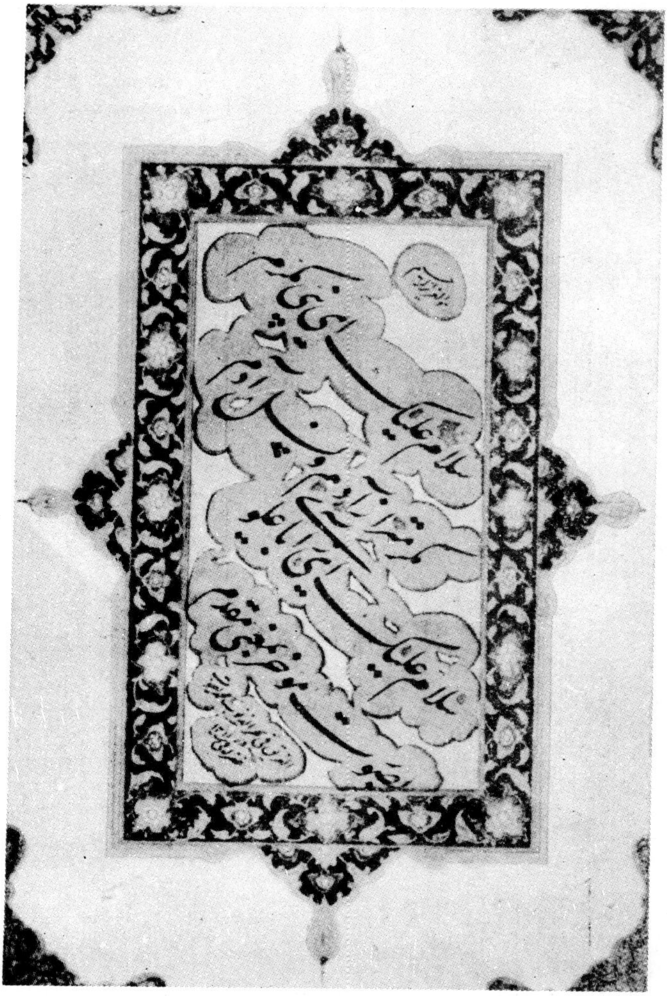

Fig. 80.

A panel of modern Nasta'liq calligraphy, by Muhammad Ya'qub of Kabul.

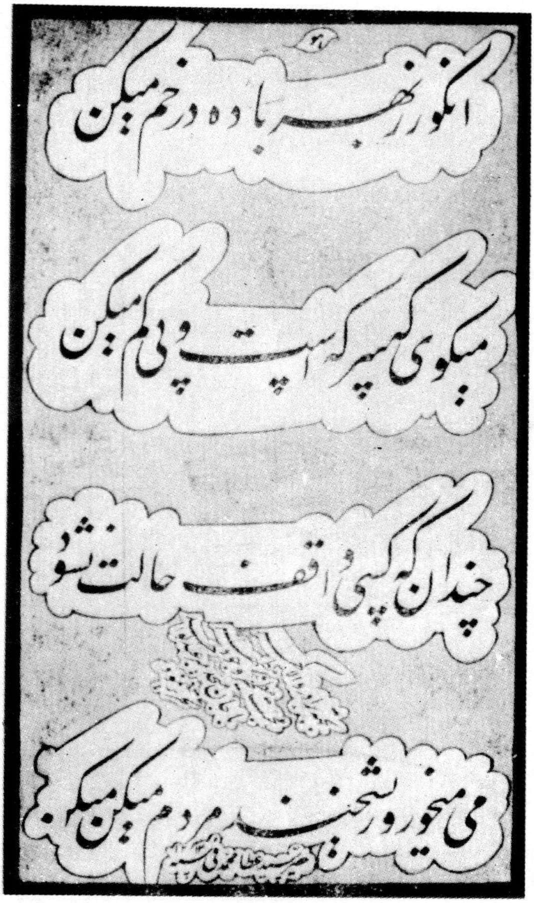

Fig. 81.

A panel of modern calligraphy, by Sayyad 'Ata Muhammad of Kabul.

be formed of the briskness of their business by looking over the number of books that some of the libraries are recorded to have contained. Harunar-Rashid's library at Baghdad, called *Baitul-Hikmat*, that is, "The Abode of Wisdom," contained ten hundred thousand books. To this library was also attached a department for translation in which scholars translated books from the Indian and Greek languages into Arabic. These translations were weighed in gold and the amount paid to the translators as wages.[1] It had separate rooms for calligraphists. This library was plundered by the Moghals. The library of Shapur bin Ardshir, the minister of Bahaud-Daulah, contained ten thousand manuscripts. This one was burnt to ashes by Tughril Baig in 447 A. H.[2] In Egypt 'Aziz Billah had collected sixteen hundred thousand works (365 A. H.). These were destroyed by Kurds.[3] The Fatimid library at Tripoli, founded by Banu 'Ammar, was the biggest that Moslems ever collected. It contained thirty hundred thousand books. It was destroyed by Christian crusaders in 502 A. H. [4] Granada had seventeen big and hundred and twenty small schools which had libraries attached to them, comprising four hundred thousand books. Eighty libraries were open for public use day and night. The royal library at Cordova occupied a whole palace.

Those who could afford sent agents to different countries for buying and copying books. Faizi had his agents in Persia. Hunain bin Ishaq had his agents in Roman countries who bought or copied for him books on Greek sciences and arts.[5] The monthly salaries he paid to his translators alone amounted to £250.[6] Muhammad bin 'Abdul Malik paid £1000 monthly to his translators. Hakam II, the Spanish king, was a great lover of books. "Never had so learned a prince reigned in Spain," writes Prof. R. Dozy, "and although all his predecessors had been men of culture, who loved to enrich their libraries, none of them had sought so eagerly for rare and precious books. At Cairo, Baghdad, Damascus and Alexandria, Hakam had agents who copied or bought for him—grudging no cost—ancient and modern manuscripts. With these treasures his place overflowed ; on all sides,

1. Fihrist, p. 243 ; Abul-Faraj, p. 146.
2. Ibn Asir, II, p 145 ; Yaqut, I, p. 799
3. Ibn Khaldun, IV, p. 81.
4. Gibbon's Roman Empire, VII, p. 505.
5. There was a regular profession of book agents or brokers of book, who were called *Dallalul Kutub*, Ibn Khallikan, I, p. 63.
6. Tabaqat ul-Atibba, I, p. 187 ; Fihrist, p. 243.

too, were to be seen copyists, binders, and illuminators." [1] And this description would also hold true for most of the houses of the literati and the rich of those days.

The standard of literacy at Baghdad was higher than that at Granada, Cordova or Nishapur. The annual expenditure of the Nizamiyyah school at Baghdad, where education was imparted free, was six hundred thousand *dinars* (£ 300,000).[2] Here education was also common among women. Among the slave girls of Zubaida, the wife of Harunar-Rashid, there were one hundred that had had proper education. [3] According to Dr. Sprenger's estimate, the number of such outstanding personalities among scholars whose lives have ben recorded in biographical works (the *Rijāl*) is about five hundred thousand.[4] The number of ordinary literate men and women must be, therefore, about a thousand times greater. While most of the literate people strove to acquire a good handwriting, an equipment very commonly desired by Moslems, how keen must have been the competition among calligraphists and how high the standard of excellence in penmanship ?

Professional artists of various branches of arts and crafts had to learn calligraphy which formed part of their decorative schemes. The gold-smith, the jeweller, the copper-and iron-smiths, the seal engraver, the wood and stone engravers and the potters were often experts in several styles of calligraphy, and they wrought their wares with inscriptions that gladdened the heart of a calligraphist.

Among innumerable scribes, the calligraphist was one who specially devoted himself to developing penmanship as an art in itself. And they were always the selected few. They copied works not so much for reproducing a text as for writing it beautifully. They displayed their art on panels of paper, called *wasli*, which fetched them handsome price. These panels were papers, mounted on card-boards, containing a poem, generally a quatrain, in bold hand, very often illuminated ; these were bought by lovers of art as works of art and students of calligraphy kept them as models for exercise.

The work of a calligraphist was always costly and greatly prized by admirers. Five hundred pounds for a book of four hundred pages was not a rare price. These artists pursued their profession with a

1. Spanish Islam, R. Dozy, p. 454; see Al-Maqrizi, I, p. 408.
2. Sirajul-Muluk, p. 267.
3. Abul-Mahasin, I, p. 632
4. Mazamin-i-Shibli, p. 35.

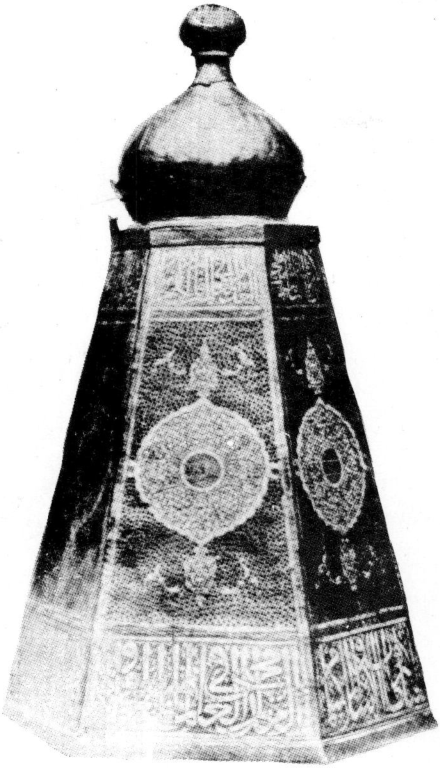

Fig. 82.

Bronze chandelier inlaid with silver, with the name of Qait Bay ; inscriptions are in decorative Nusk, XV century (Victoria and Albert Museum).

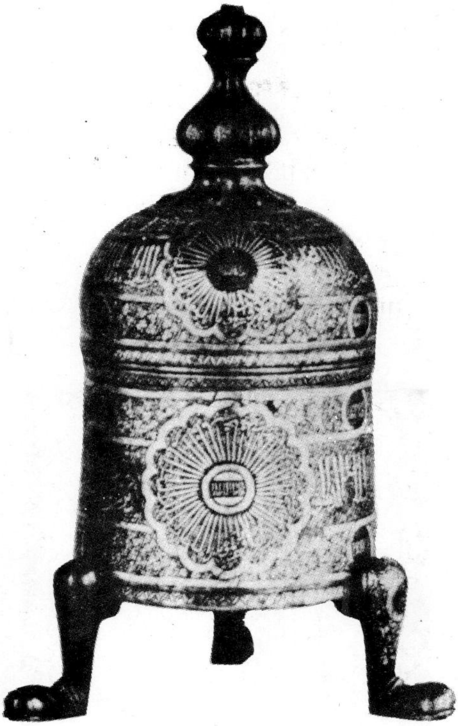

Fig. 83.

Bronze incense-burner inlaid with silver, bearing the name of Muhammad Ibn Qalaun ; the inscriptions are in decorative Suls style ; XIV century (Victoria & Albert Museum).

devotion almost ascetic and imposed on themselves strict discipline. We often read that such and such a calligraphist never omitted his daily exercise of writing a few pages till the very day he expired. They were in fact revered in their society as saints and were often men of strong moral purity and religious character.

Ghulam Muhammad, Haft Qalami (i. e. 'the master of seven styles') was particularly keen on visiting calligraphists personally. His meeting with another calligraphist and the love with which they talked about their profession should be of interest here. The Haft Qalami, on hearing the fame of Hafiz Nurullah, went to see him. Even on his first visit he found him extremely well-mannered, unassuming, just and absolutely devoid of pride. "The Hafiz," writes the Haft Qalami, "showed me his papers of exercise. He had, by then, transcribed the ***Haft-band-i-Kashi***, at the request of Asafud Daula Bahadur. How would I put in words the miracle the Hafiz had performed with his pen ? It was verily a garden in full blossom ! No body would ever be satisfied by looking at it. A long time passed in looking and enjoying these papers . . . without any exaggeration I may say that this noble heart, notwithstanding the greatness he has attained in his art, has no pride whatsoever. . . ."

They then talked of Shahjahanabad, and the Hafiz asked : "I have heard, Sir, that you have brought with yourself the calligraphy of Aqa 'Abdur Rashid. Would you be indeed so kind as to allow me to illuminate my eyes by having a look at them ?" Next time the Haft Qalami took the specimens of the Aqa's writing with him. "The Hafiz was extremely delighted by seeing both the bold and the fine varieties of the Aqa's penmanship. From morning till after the noon he looked at them. . . . "[1]

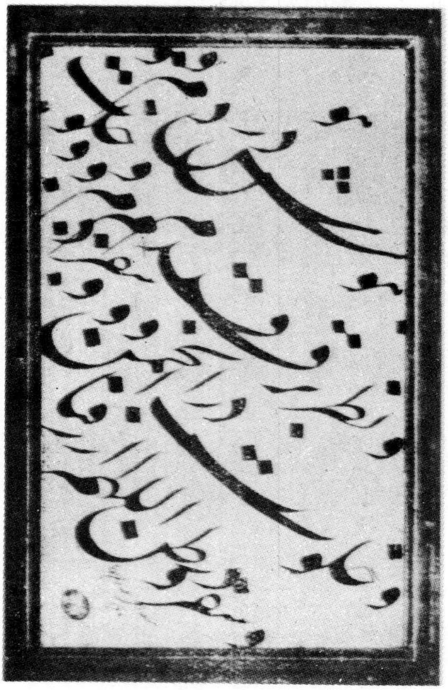

Fig. 84.
A specimen showing how an artist practises strokes and curves, by 'Abdur Rahman of Herat.

Their art absorbed all their attention and they were generally respected by all, alike by kings and the people. And calligraphists, too, were well aware of their importance, and were not always so very humble and unassuming as the Haft Qalami found the Hafiz to be. A few examples illustrative of the honour they enjoyed would not be out of place here.

Mir Khalilullha Shah was greatly honoured in his days. He copied the '*Nau-Ras* with great care and made a present of it to Ibrahim 'Adil Shah, the king of the Deccan. The King was extremely pleased with the gift and the accomplishment of the artist. He bestowed on him the title of "The king of the pen", and as a mark of extraordinary honour made him sit on his throne. After this ceremony was over, he bade his courtiers to accompany him to his residence.[2]

1. Tazkira-i-Khushnawisan, pp. 45, 46.
2. Ibid, pp. 79, 80.

The Haft Qalami writes that an admirer of Khalilullah Shah's calligraphy wanted to buy some of his papers for seven hundred rupees, but the owner would not sell. After much haggling the bargain was struck for an Arabian horse. The customer procured one and bought the papers.[1]

Yaqut Musta'sami (1203 A. D.) has been considered the greatest of Naskh writers. His reputation was so great that even in his lifetime books copied by him had spread all over the Moslem world. Each of his copies of the dictionary *al-jauhari* was sold at hundred *dinars* (£ 50).[2] He once copied the *Shafa* of Avecenna and sent the same to Muhammad Tughlaq (1324 A.D.) in India. The King appreciated the work greatly and sent to the calligraphist a gift of two hundred million *misqals* of gold in return. But the artist refused the gift considering it beneath his dignity to accept such a meagre sum.[3]

Mir 'Imadal-Husaini of Qazwin, the unapproachable master of the Nasta'liq style was almost a martyr to the pride he had in his talent. He cared little for the money and honour that was lavished on him so abundantly. Shah 'Abbas Safawi (1587/1629 A.D.) asked him to copy the *Shah-Namah* of Firdausi, that stupendous epic, and along with the request he sent him the meagre sum of seventy *tumans*. After the lapse of a year, the king sent for the book. Mir 'Imad handed the messenger seventy lines from the beginning of the book, and told the messenger that for the gift of the Shah this was all he could offer. This remark offended the king, who sent back those seventy lines to the calligraphist, and demanded his gold back. The Mir was up to the occasion again. He took a pair of scissors and neatly cut those lines into seventy pieces. Each piece he gave to a disciple of his, who went home and brought back a *tuman* with him. Mir 'Imad then counted up seventy *tumans* in the palm of the messenger. He

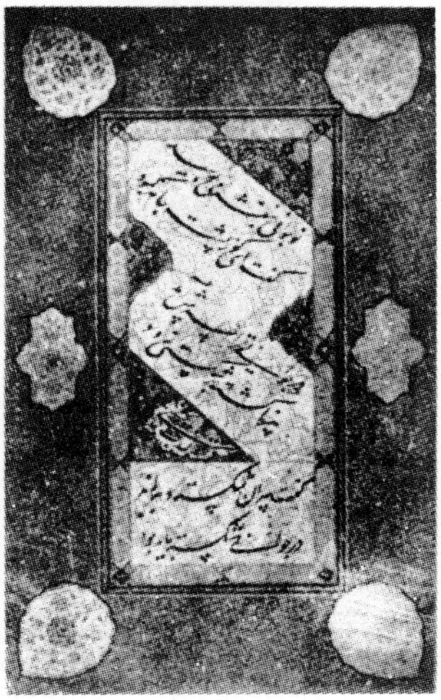

Fig. 85.
A panel of Mir 'Imad's Nasta'liq calligraphy

1. Ibid, p. 81.
2. Ibn Khallikan, p. 207.
3. Les Calligraphes et les Miniaturistes, Huart, p. 85.

was murdered shortly after this event, in 1615 A. D. ; the crime is said to have been committed at the instigation of the king himself.[1]

Mir 'Imad's calligraphy was very much admired by Shah Jahan. He gave the title of *Yak-sadi* (centurion) to every one who presented him a specimen of his writing.[2]

Among the last of the great penmen the work of Aqa 'Abdur-Rashid was most dearly valued by the lovers of the art. He was a cousin and a student of Mir 'Imad. He came to India in Shah Jahan's time and was appointed a teacher to the prince Dara Shikoh, whom he instructed in the Nasta'liq style. Most of his life he passed at Akbarabad and was also buried there after his death. His calligraphy came to be so highly valued and so rare that those who possessed specimens were afraid of exhibiting them, lest they lose them.

The name of a renowned calligraphist meant money to forgers and they have exploited some great names, in particular the students of renowned artists. For example, a pupil of Aqa 'Abdur-Rashid, named Amir Razwi, imitated his style and signed his own writings by the Aqa's name. The Haft Qalami remarks, it required a very careful examination to decide which was which. The death anniversary of Aqa 'Abdur-Rashid was regularly observed in the month of Muharram, at Akbarabad. Calligraphists of all the important towns in the neighbourhood, specially those of Delhi, attended it, and benefited by exchanging their views on their art and other professional matters. A more lively gathering, however, was held on the fourth of every month at the house of Shah Waris 'Ali. He was a good calligraphist and specialized in the decorative style called *Gulzar* and also in the Shikasta hand. He was a lively soul and by no means over religious. In the monthly meetings that were held at his place, he entertained his visitors with music and dance by dancing girls. The Haft Qalami says that this meeting was always a great success. Shah Waris 'Ali died in 1227 A. H.[3]

Maulana Khawja Muhammad too had the same habit of signing his writings by the name of his master, the celebrated artist Mullah Mir 'Ali. Few People could detect the difference. His master was aware of the havoc his student had done and was still doing. He has complained of this misfortune of his in a poem, wherein he says :

---

1. Tazkirah-i-Khushnawisan, pp. 92, 93.
2. Ibid, p. 93.
3. Ibid, p. 131.

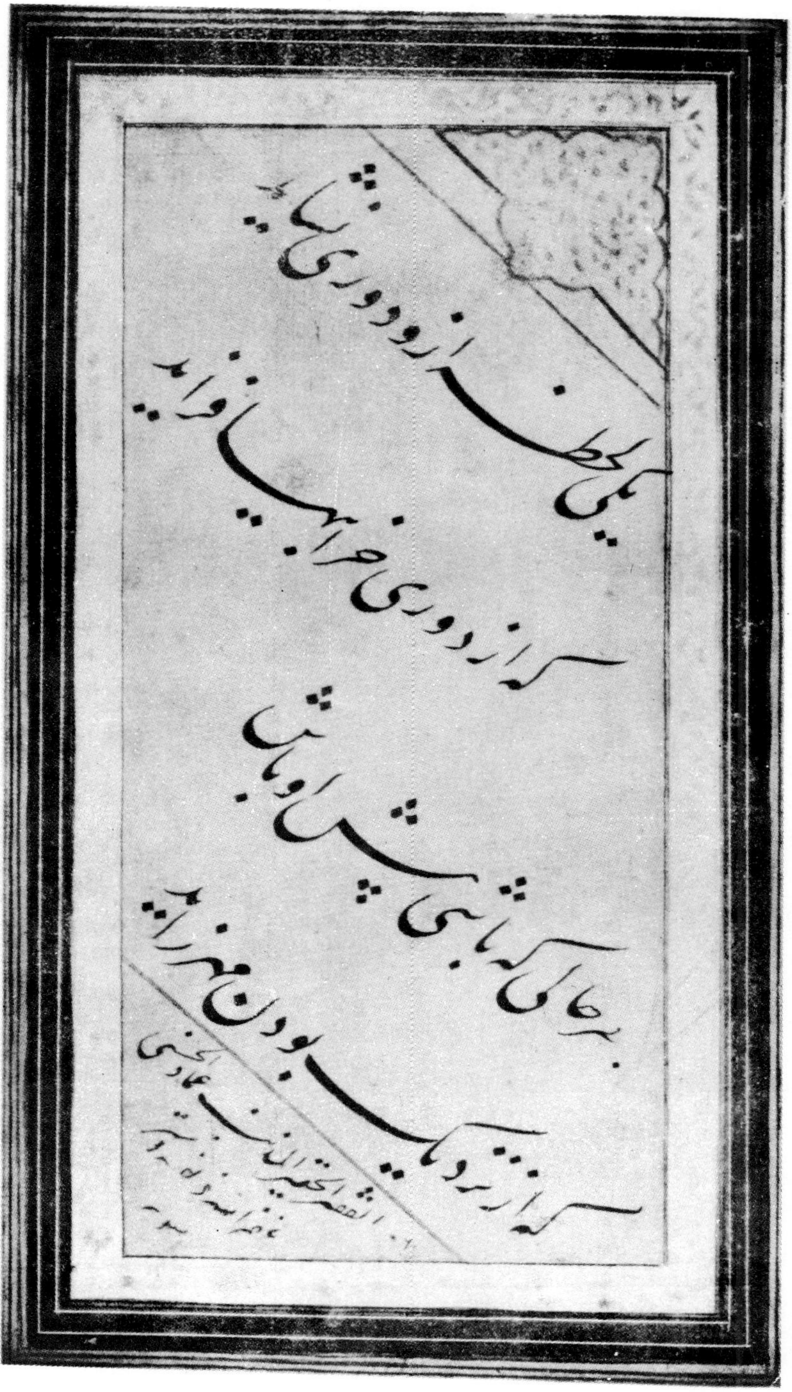

Fig. 86.
A panel of the calligraphy of the celebrated 'Imadal-Husaini of Qazwin
(reproduced with gratitude from the Moslem Review of April 1936).

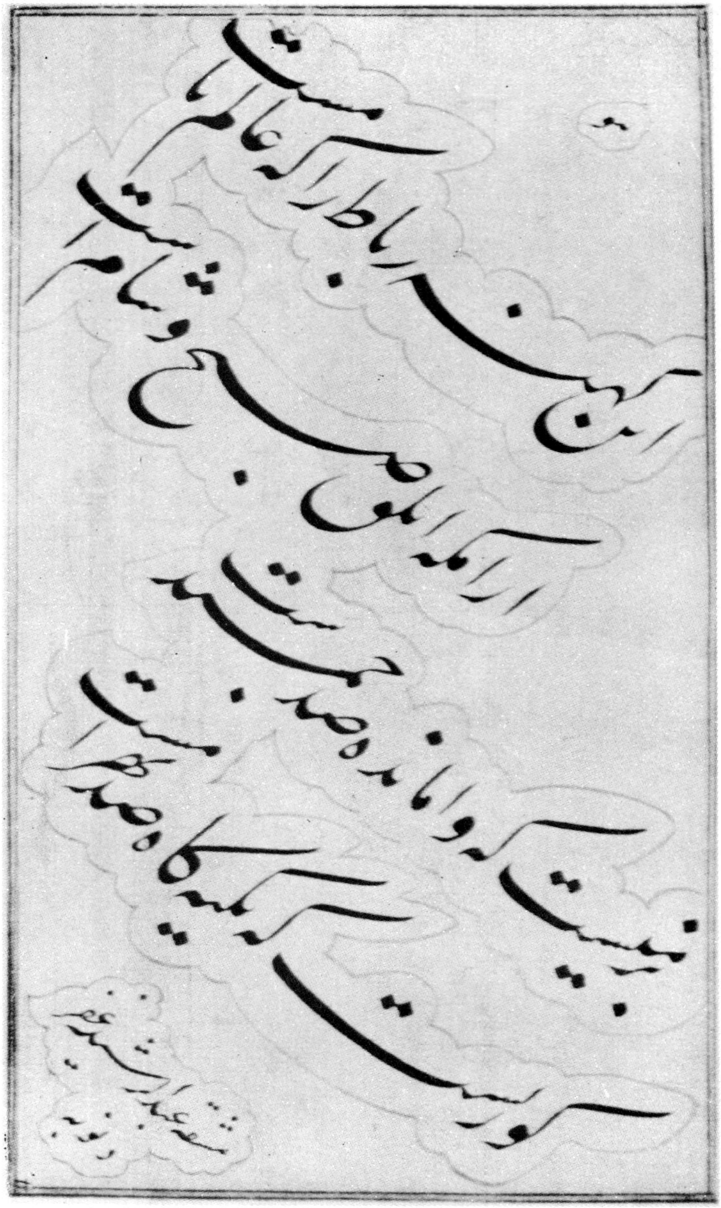

Fig. 87.
An extraordinarily beautiful specimen of Aqa 'Abdur-Rashid's calligraphy (reproduced with gratitude from the Moslem Review).

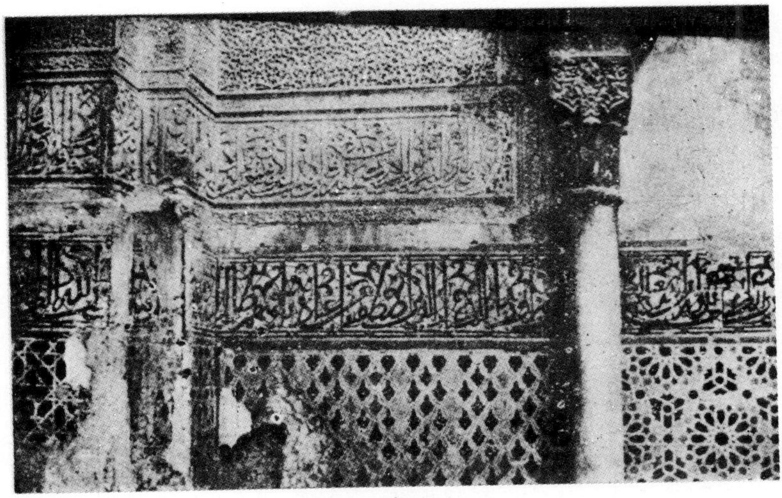

Fig. 88.
A band of inscription in the decorative Suls of the western variety, in mosaic faience, Madrasatul-'Attarin̄, Fez.

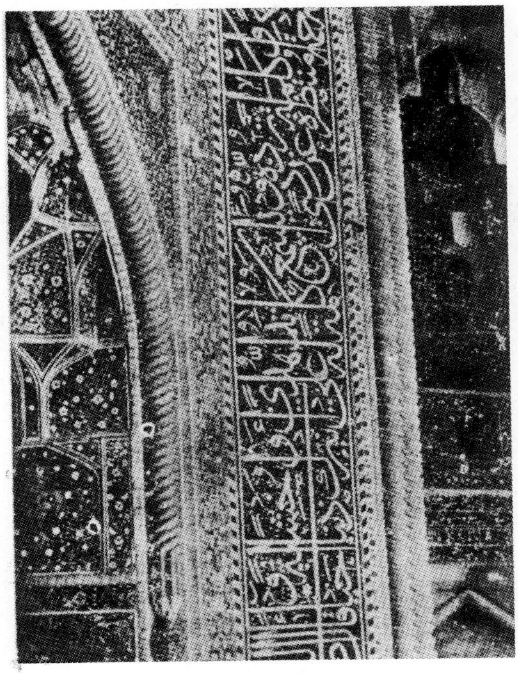

Fig. 89.
Architrave of the Masjid-i-Shah, Isfahan ; the inscription in the decorative Naskh style, done in mosaic faience.

"Khawjah Mahamud was my disciple for sometime, and I tried my best to instruct him, till his handwriting developed a feature. I have done him no wrong, nor does he do me any, save that he writes good or bad as best he can and signs the lot in my name."[1]

Jahangir was an admirer of Mullah Mir 'Ali's hand ; the Mir himself was conscious of his talents and he has made no secret of it. In his poems he has often referred to the superiority of his art. A poem of his, of which I give a translation here, is remarkable in the sense that it describes that subtle point in the art of calligraphy where it touches pure art :

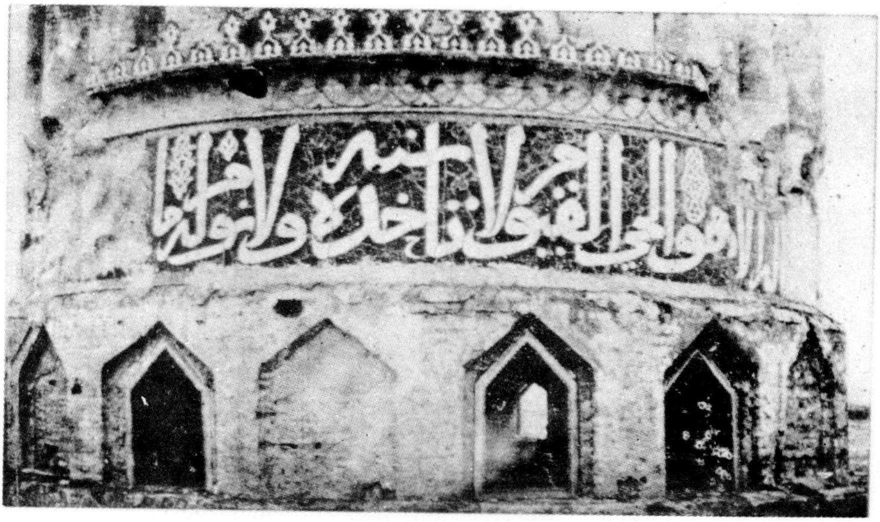

Fig. 90.

Mausoleum of Princess Tughai (d. 1348), the drum of its dome, with the inscription in Suls style of the Western variety, in mosaic faience, Cairo.

"My pen works miracles, and rightly enough is the *form* of my words proud of its superiority over its *meaning*. To each of the curves of my letters the heavenly vault confesses its bondage in slavery, and the value of each of my strokes is eternity itself."[2]

---

1. Tazkira-i-Khushnawisan, p. 80.
2. Ibid, p. 52.

III

NASKH AND OTHER STYLES

Of the two main off-shoots or elementary styles of the original Arabic script, viz. the cursive and the angular, the latter, because of its monumental character, came to be selected as the preferred script of the government. And, in obedience to the general tendency in art during the period of Arab predominance, the calligraphist too tried his best to bring out its ornamental possibilities. This script, that is, the angular Kufic, had absorbed the attention of the artists to the almost complete neglect of the cursive variety, until in its progress on ornamental lines, it departed so far away from its original structure that it failed to serve its primary purpose as the script of a language.

In the meanwhile, the common cursive variety of the Kufic continued to be used for common and less artistic purposes—for the copying of books of common use and correspondence, where lack of embellishment was not of much consequence. After about three centuries of monopoly as the preferred script of the Moslem world, the Kufic lost its ground. For about two centuries more it was used, almost exclusively, for ornamental purposes and then became obsolete. The round variety, which had been developing unnoticed, under the long shadow of the lordly Kufic, came to be recognised as the script of the State. It was given the distinctive name of Naskh. It had incorporated into itself all those orthographical improvements that had been worked out in the Kufic, and appeared on the stage of art fully dressed with vowel-marks, punctuation and diacritical signs.

The advent of the Naskh style brought in an important period of renaissance in the history of Moslem calligraphy. So far the Kufic had been mostly cultivated not so much for its own sake as for the decorative scheme to which it lent itself so easily. The script had become subservient to an ulterior motive, the decoration of a surface. With the Naskh appeared the tendency to realize the grace latent in the script itself; that is, the writing, and not the ornamental rhythm it could display, became the object of calligraphy. It was realized, in strong reaction to the ornamental Kufic, that the artist must remain

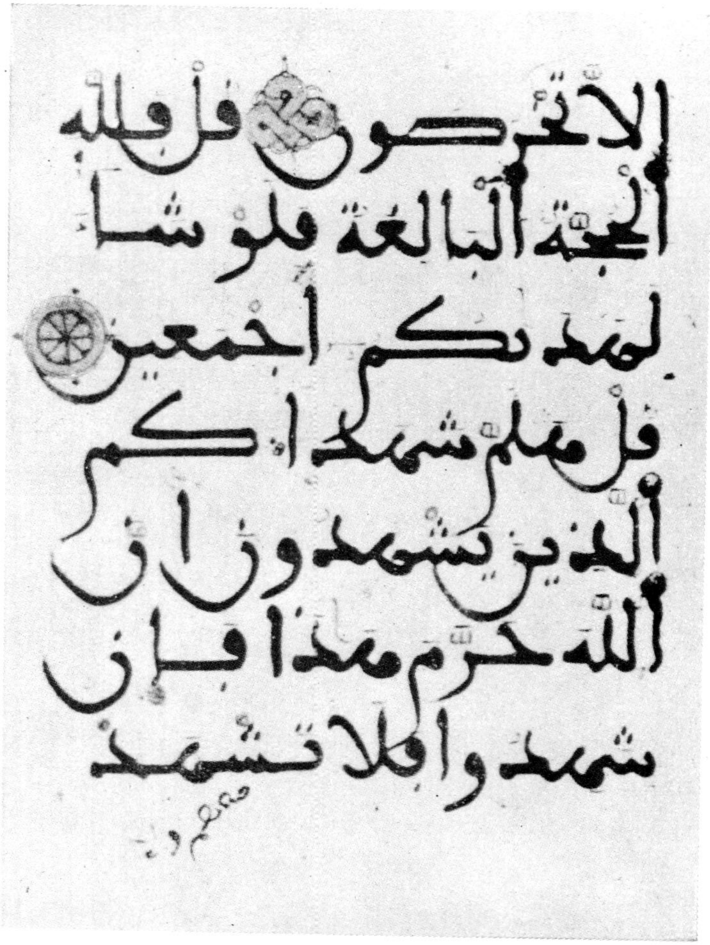

Fig. 91.

A specimen of the early Naskh, developing out of the round variety of the Kufic, which marked the period of transition from the Kufic to the Naskh.

faithful to the genuine features of the script ; he must not violate the original form of his script.

But a script has no original character inasmuch as it is not a natural object. One can never be sure of being quite faithful to the original form, which form, if it ever had one at the moment of its birth, has been lost beyond recovery. A script is an invention of man, an artificial means of expressing an idea ; a purely intellectual contrivance. This, however, does not seem to be the view the calligraphist holds on the matter. To him his script is a living thing and, as such, though it undergoes changes as it grows and becomes more and more aged, it always has some features, peculiar to its age, which are its genuine features and people know it by those features. The calligraphist watches its growth in the hands of the people. And to this living medium of his art he wishes to remain faithful. And yet, if the artist were to simply copy the script as he has received it from the hands of the masses he would not be faithful to his profession, and would not be doing his job. He must make the writing look beautiful. To attain this purpose he must change, however slightly, the proportions of strokes and curves that go to make the features of his script.

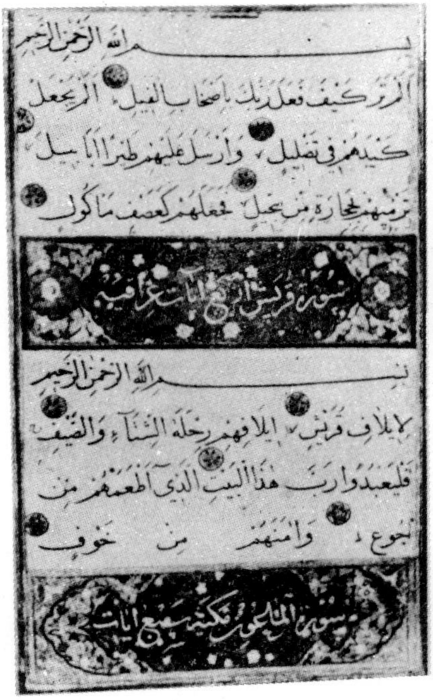

Fig. 92.
A page from a Koran MS. of the XIII century.

This the calligraphist does by taking into account the tendencies that are working towards the gradual change of the script and by taking into confidence the fancy of his readers. That is, he changes the forms of his letters after their liking. He follows the way the masses of his readers are sure to appreciate. By modifying the form of letters he makes them simpler of execution. He changes angles into rounder curves and lets strokes follow the natural sweep of the hand. Thus, while the identity of the letter is not lost, the writing is made easier, more to the taste of the readers and beautiful. In bringing about a change of this nature, the calligraphist depends more upon the change of the proportion of curves and strokes than on any thing else. By changing these proportions he gives different expressions to letters without interfering with the outlines of their anatomy, their orthography.

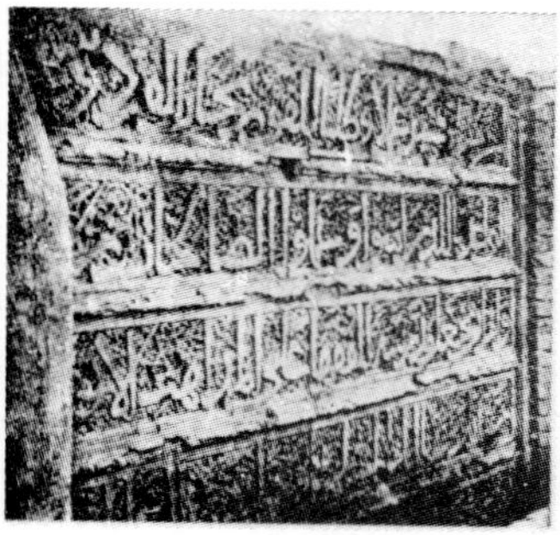

Fig. 93.
Naskh inscription carved at Mustansiriyyah, Baghdad.

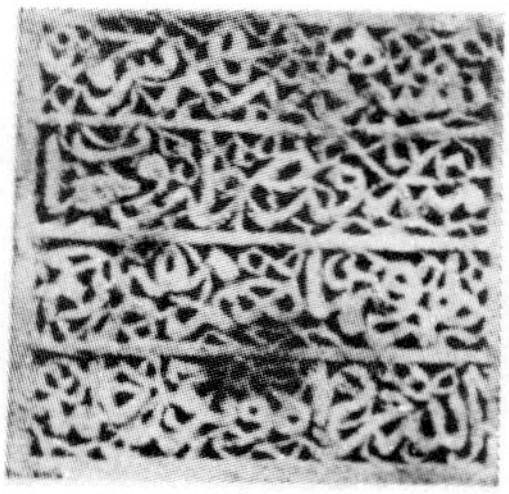

Fig. 94.
Naskh inscription carved in stone, Baghdad.

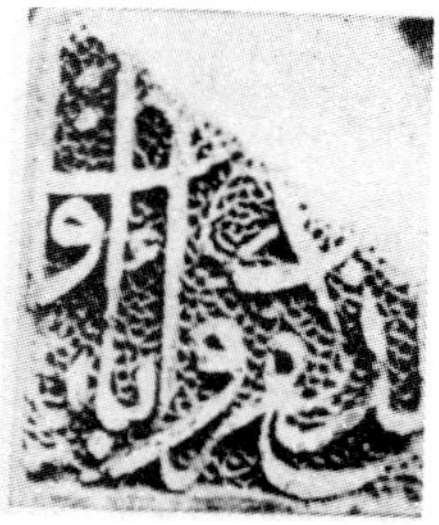

Fig. 95.
Fragment of a Naskh inscription carved in stone, Baghdad

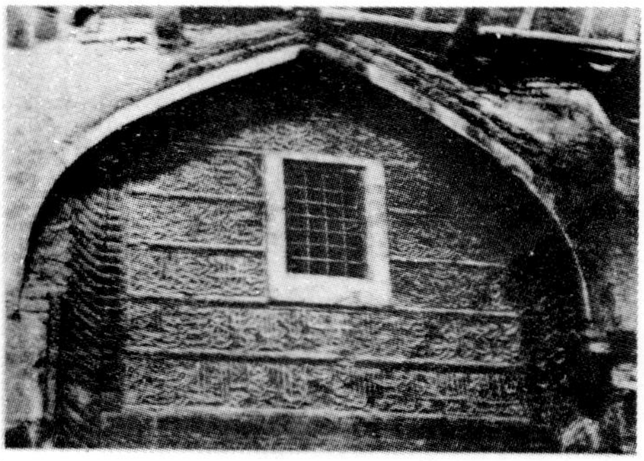

Fig. 96.
Naskh inscription at Khan Artmah, Baghdad

Through a gradual change in the artistic as well as the utilitarian improvement of the script, scores of newer styles developed. Most of them were lost as they did not develop into styles of any marked distinction and stable value, or because they were products of pure fancy and served no useful purpose. Many of them were nothing more than ingenious, and their ornamental merits did not suit the utility of art. It was this defect which had proved suicidal in the case of the ornamental Kufic. The calligraphist never risked his art that way again. For the display of ingenuity and ornamental fancy, he had to take recourse to certain styles that were set apart for this purpose, viz. the Gulzar, the Tughra, the Ta'us and the Zulf-i-'urus, etc. From the Kufic down to Nasta'liq—the latest and the simplest of styles—the tendency has been from the complicated and angular to the more

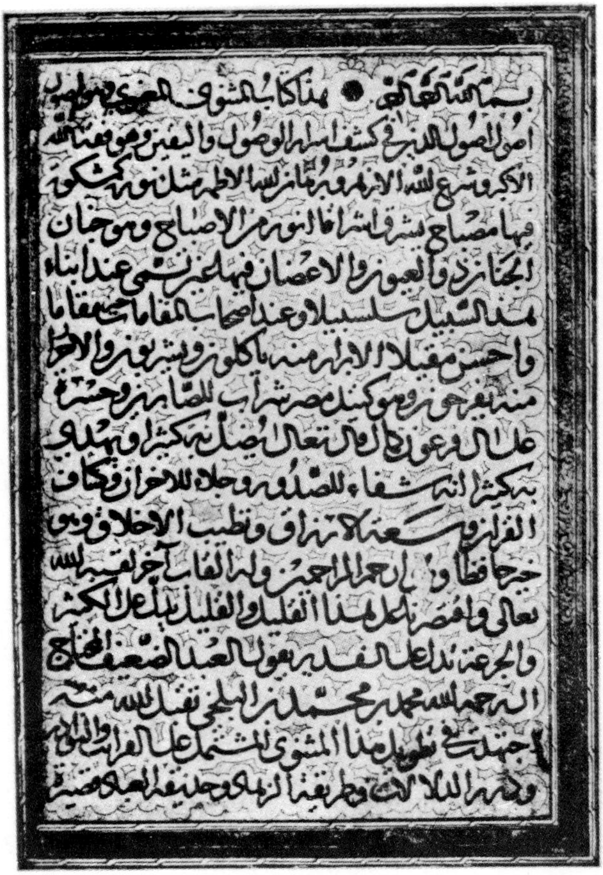

Fig. 97.

A page from the Masnawi of Jalaluddin Rumi, in decorative Naskh, XV century, Persia.

round. Only in the special ornamental and monumental styles the calligraphist indulges in ingenuity and complication.

The ideal of a calligraphist, like that of the adepts in other arts, was to express an emotion, which he strove to realize through the medium of the linear rhythm that his script was capable of producing. While every man and woman can walk, only a few of them can walk elegantly ; any one might be able to write but few can make letters dance with grace.

The charm of a calligraphic writing is contained in the structure of strokes and curves which aim at producing a graceful movement instinct with universal appeal. A painter by his keen study of

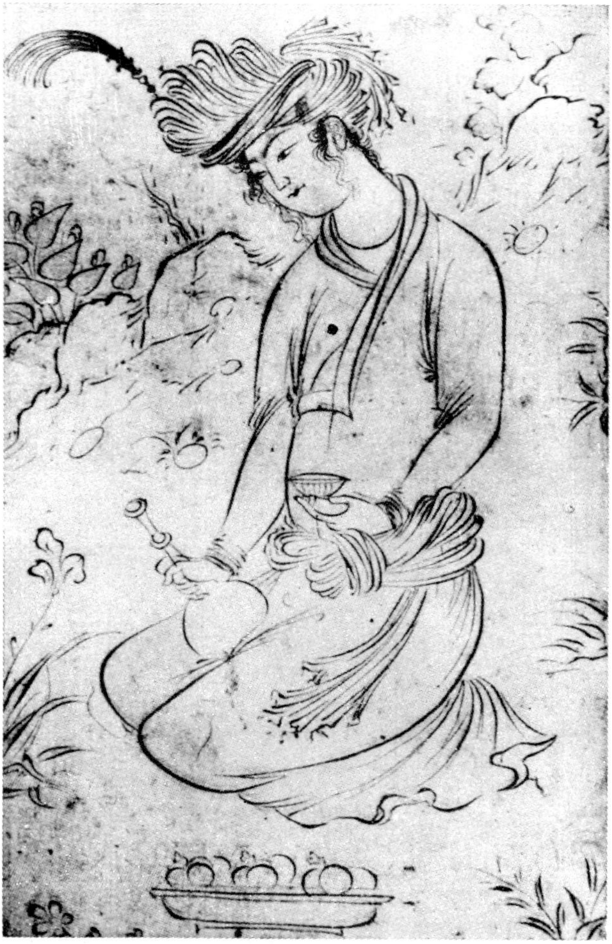

Fig. 98.
Calligraphic drawing of a Persian lady, XV century, Persia.

expressions portrays in human faces joy, grief, anger, peace, or disgust by making use of certain lines that are suggestive of such emotions. A line, by its nature, is symbolic of a movement, of a particular rhythm abstracted from a natural object. A calligraphist selects a particular kind of line which he feels would produce the desired suggestion. His success depends upon the successful execution of the theme of his rhythm. Styles in calligraphy differ from each other in the styles of rhythm they convey.

Calligraphists succeeded so much in catching the spirit of the rhythm of life in their writing that painters, particularly of the fifteenth century, adopted the technique of the calligraphist for their art.

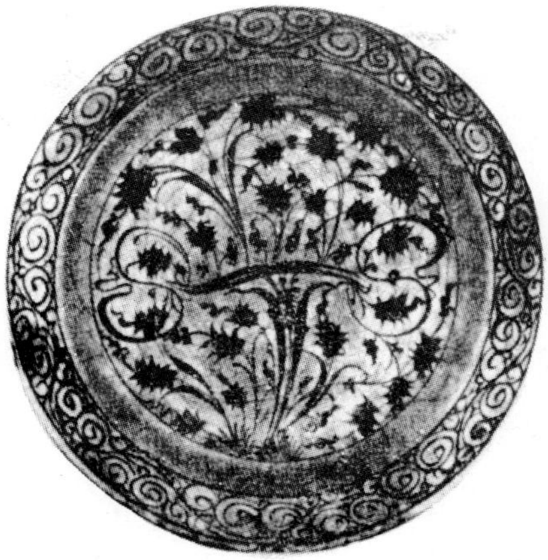

Fig. 99.

In a human drawing of calligraphic nature (Fig. 98), lines are suggestive of a joyous play of the moulding outlines of the human body. Without taking the help of shades, a line by gradually growing to a suitable breadth towards the centre, in the form of a muscle or a muscle fibre, suggests the roundness of a limb and seems to be full with the property of life. A line of this or a similar description has been defined by Mr. Huges as a 'beauty-line'; and a calligraphist selects this kind of line for his writing. The example of the 'beauty line' that Mr. Huges has given is similar to the two lines running horizontally in the middle of the plate shown above (Fig. 99).

This drawing on a glazed plate is calligraphic inasmuch as it symbolizes the rhythm of the growth of a luxuriant plant. It represents the dance of vegetable life, the dream of a plant. Lines used in this drawing are similar to those used in the ink-drawing of a Persian lady (Fig. 98). They suggest, apart from their

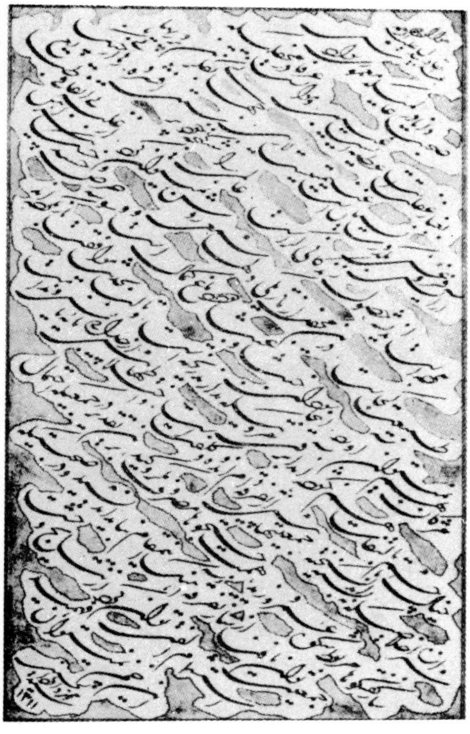

Fig. 100.
Shikasta-amiz style, calligraphed by S. Muhammad Da'ud al-Husaini.

subject, a particular rhythm of life, a more or less abstract way of representing an emotion. The beauty and the rhythm that a calligraphist strives to realize is similar to these drawings but much more abstract in subject.

Dr. Upham Pope, rightly ascribing to calligraphy the perfection that ink-drawing had attained in Persia, observes: ". . . The Persians'

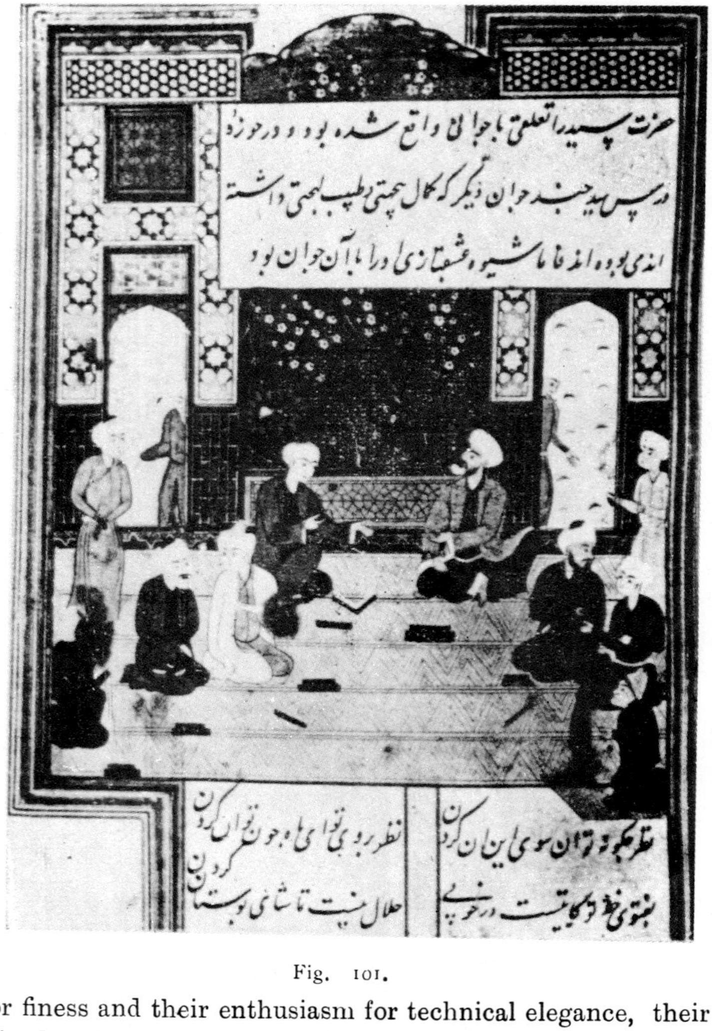

Fig. 101.

love for finess and their enthusiasm for technical elegance, their long-disciplined and instructed sense for the flowing line learned from calligraphy, were among the several influences that converged to carry the art of drawing to a very high rank. . . . Some of the fifteenth century drawings of the Herat school are essentially compositions in calli-

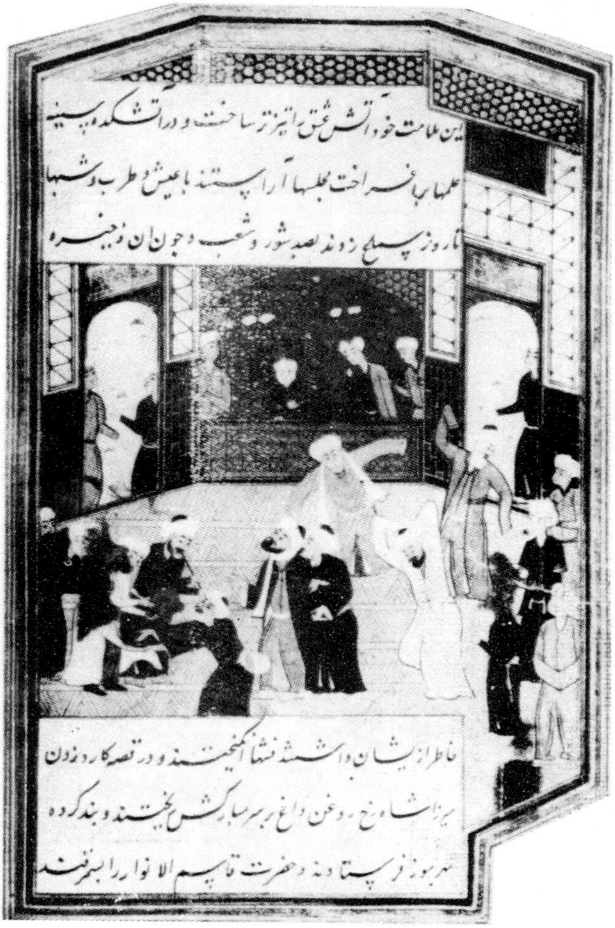

Fig. 102.

graphic strokes, and each line is endowed with a lovely and expressive grace that could only have been the product of a sophisticated passion for calligraphy."[1]

Another factor which we must take into account is the influence of the Chinese and the Manichaean or the Central-Asian art on both the calligraphy and painting of Persia. In Central-Asian art line-drawing of calligraphic style had reached its perfection, long before the Persians began to experiment in it. Such drawings appear in Persia with the invasions of Mongols and Turks. These people were

1. An Introduction to Persian Art, p. 115.

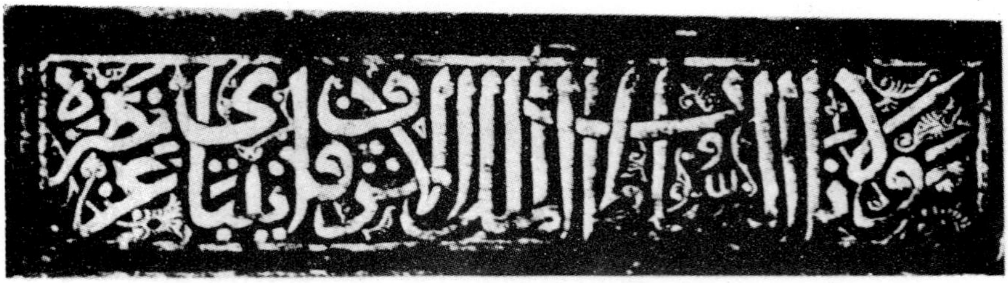

Fig. 103.
An ivory panel carved with a Naskh inscription XV century, Cairo.

familiar with the Chinese ink-drawings in Buddhist temples, and also with Chinese calligraphy done in frescoes on temple walls, on silk and porcelain. China silk and porcelain, however, had entered Persia earlier than the invasions of the Mongols.[1]

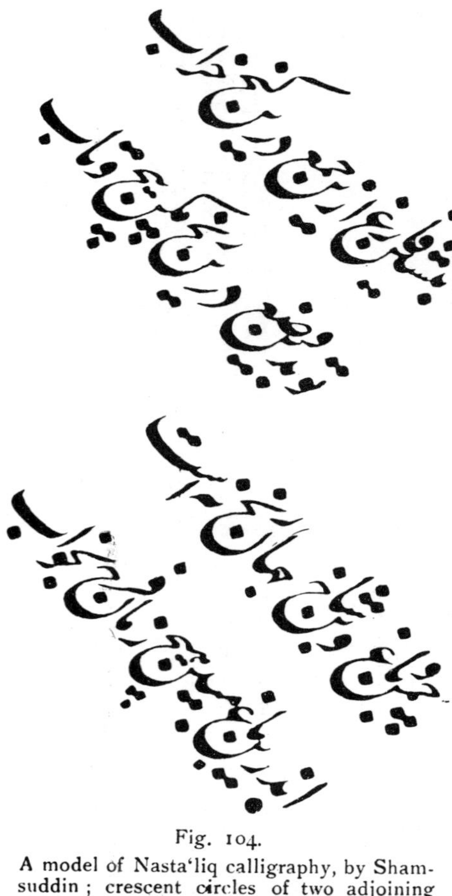

Fig. 104.
A model of Nasta'liq calligraphy, by Shamsuddin ; crescent circles of two adjoining words are made to merge into one.

To return to calligraphy proper, I wish to point out that apart from the main styles that developed as off-shoots of Naskh, every master, in whatever style he wrote, had an individual style of his own. As a student of calligraphy strove to imitate his model, his practice, in case he had talent, developed into an improved style. Such individual artists provide us with innumerable styles within styles, infinite shades of emotion and qualities. It is often difficult to detect such individual variations. While we may feel them it is not always possible to lay our finger on the subtle distinctions.

In order to develop a particular trait in his style, an artist makes the most of his energies both physical and mental. He might

1. Islamic Culture, Jan. 1931, p. 40 ; Oct. p. 64.

strive to make his handwriting firm and bold, expressive of strength, or rough, or austere, or exquisitely delicate, graceful and sweet. Whatever be the nature of the conscious attempt of the artist at bringing out a particular shade of character, it must be admitted that most of his distinctive qualities are the result of the stress his subconscious mind has on his art. His peculiarities reflect his personality, his mental character, which discipline and practice bring out in fine shades. It is extremely difficult to point out such mental qualities of a writing with any degree of precision, much less to analyze them. Analysis of the handwriting of a master would amount to the analysis of his mind which is always baffling.

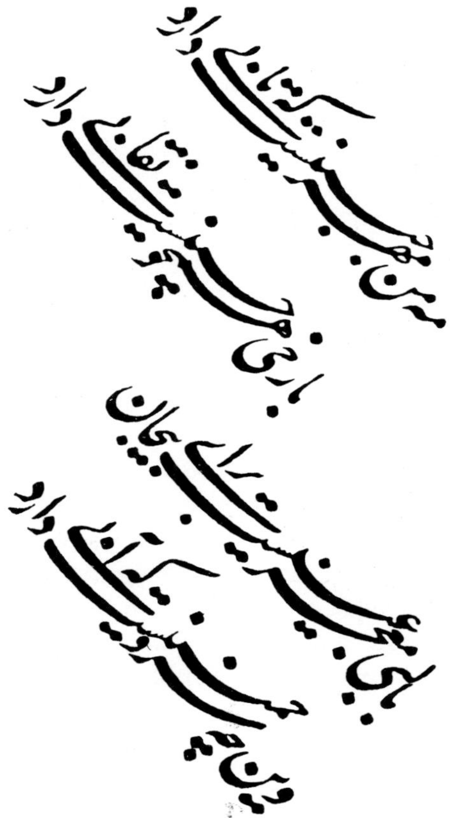

Fig. 105.
A model for exercise in Nasta'liq calligraphy, by Shamsuddin, showing the symmetrical arrangement of similar strokes.

Today we do not possess that passion which older generations had for a good handwriting ; and we have no idea what amount of labour is required in mastering a stroke that might pass as fairly good. Consequently, we do not possess any real criterion with which we might be able to judge a work of calligraphy. We lack that sympathy which comes through practical acquaintance with the art. We might greatly admire a writing but our admiration is bound to be superficial, because it is of the uninitiated in the art. We cannot but overlook many good points of merit which personal touch with the pen can alone reveal.

The Naskh style holds a mediate position between the Kufic and the Nasta'liq. The Naskh retains, however slightly, the suggestion of its angular origin ; its curves are never perfectly round or oval which is the peculiarity of the Nasta'liq. The stages which the Naskh passed in its development towards Nasta'liq, are marked by such styles as Suls, and Riqa'. The Naskh in itself represents the cursive Kufic softened to broader curves and freer sweeps. Fragments of the papyri published in the *Archiv Orientali* for Oct. 1935, will at a glance convince us that what was called Naskh was in fact the cursive variety of the Kufic in its developed form. It usurped the hieratic position of the Kufic and has retained it since then. The Koran is never written in Nasta'liq hand. Nasta'liq is peculiar to the Persian and the Indian. Naskh is mostly used by Arabic speaking people.

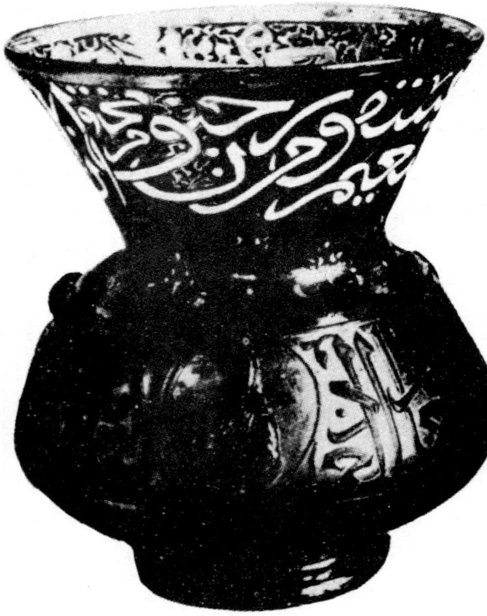

Fig. 106.

Gilt and enamelled glass mosque lamp, with Naskh inscription in white (upper) and blue (below); XIV. century.

Naskh developed different forms in different countries. The one known generally as Maghribi, i. e. 'the Western', is the earliest variety and is drawn directly from the Kufic of the 3rd century A. H., independent of the later Naskh styles. This Maghribi variety of the Arabic script, was originally known as Qairwani, Qairwan being the name of the capital of the Aghlabids (800-909 A. D.). This town was the centre of the then civilized Africa and from here this first Naskh or the first variation of the cursive Kufic spread in its neighbourhood.[1]

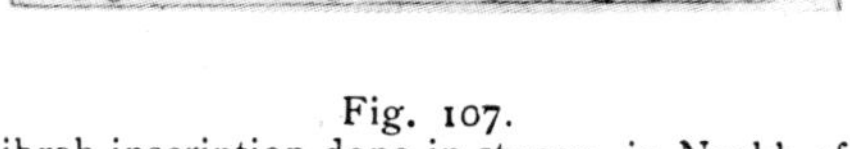

Fig. 107.
Mihrab inscription done in stucco, in Naskh of the Ayyubide period, Sinjar.

It varies from the Eastern Naskh, as the example (fig. 108) given below, would show, in the proportion of its circles that are wider in circumference, with slanting strokes flung swiftly as in Shikasta.

1. Ibn Khaldun, I. pp. 350—3.

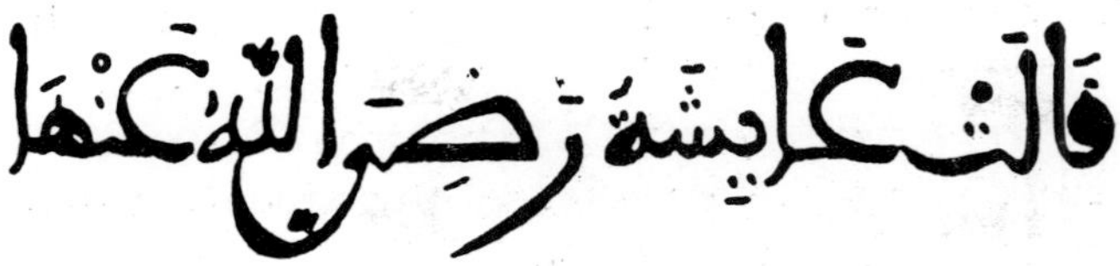

Fig. 108.
The Qairwani style.

In Spain another form of the Naskh, called Andalusian or Cardovan, came into existence. It was rounder in its curves than the Qairwani. Inscriptions on the walls of Alhambra, excluding the Kufic,

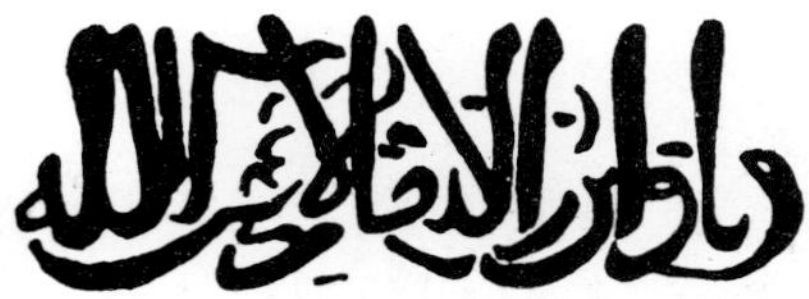

Fig. 109.
The Andalusian Naskh.

are written in the monumental Andalusian style (figs. 6, 7, 8, 109). It flourished till the fall of the Almohades in Spain.[1]

Fez evolved its Fasi style which was still rounder than the Algerian variety of the Naskh (figs. 23, 88, 110). In central Africa, at Timbakto appeared a style called Sudani. Its letters were large and thick, round or angular. The Tunisian and the Algerian styles did

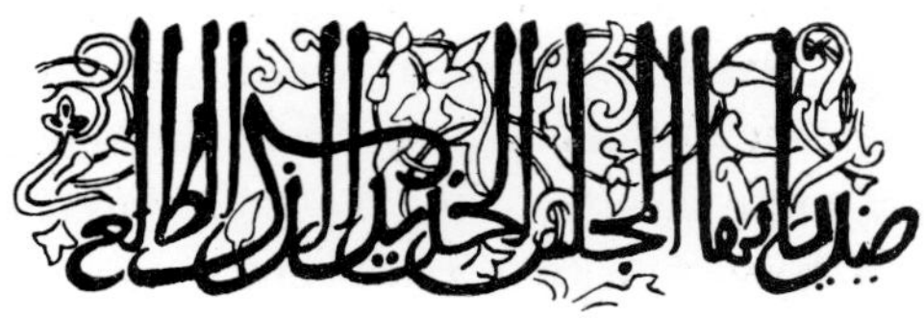

Fig. 110.
Fasi of the 14th century A. D. from a frieze on the door of a Moroccan home.

not differ from the general Western style in any remarkable degree. Although the Western style is the earliest departure from the Kufic, its oldest example dates only about 300/900 A. D.

The earliest inscription in Nasta'liq is probably that of the "Persian Deed for Sale of Land" discovered by Dr. Hoernle, and

---

1. Ibid. I. p. [illegible]51.

published by D. S. Margoliouth.[1] A digit in the date that it bears is not clearly legible. Margoliouth reads 401/1010-1011 A. D. This document bears certain proof of the fact that Nasta'liq style existed and was practiced long before this deed was written. Another Persian inscription carved in relief on the wall of an ancient mosque in Armenia (Arze-Rum), discovered and published by Belin,[2] dated 351/960 A. D., although written after the Kufic style does not successfully conceal the fact that the round (Naskh or Nasta'liq) style has been faked to look like the angular Kufic.

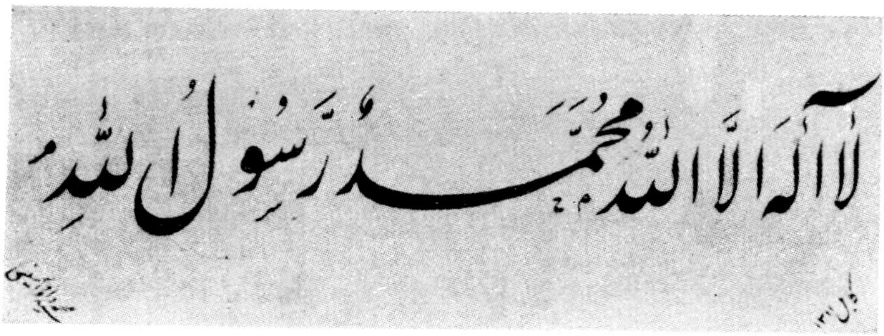

Fig. 111.

A specimen of modern Nasta'liq, confession of the Moslem faith, by Muhammad Da'ud al Husaini, Kabul.

It is true, though it sounds rather curious, that the Kufic prevailed in Persia longer than it did even in Arabia. The round Nasta'liq was developed by the Persian. Its final horizontal flourishes are considered to have been the result of the long habit of writing in the Pahlavi script that prevailed in Persia before the Arabs raided the country. Though the Nasta'liq style came into being much earlier, books were written in it only in the 13th century A. D. Persian poetical works were first copied in it. However, the habit of copying the Koran and scientific works in the Naskh and the interlinear translations and marginal commentaries in the Nasta'liq, proves that the Nasta'liq style must have become more popular in Persia than the Naskh at a very early stage of its development.

---

1. JRAS. Oct. 1903, p. 761.
2. Journal Asiatique, 1852. p. 376, plate II.

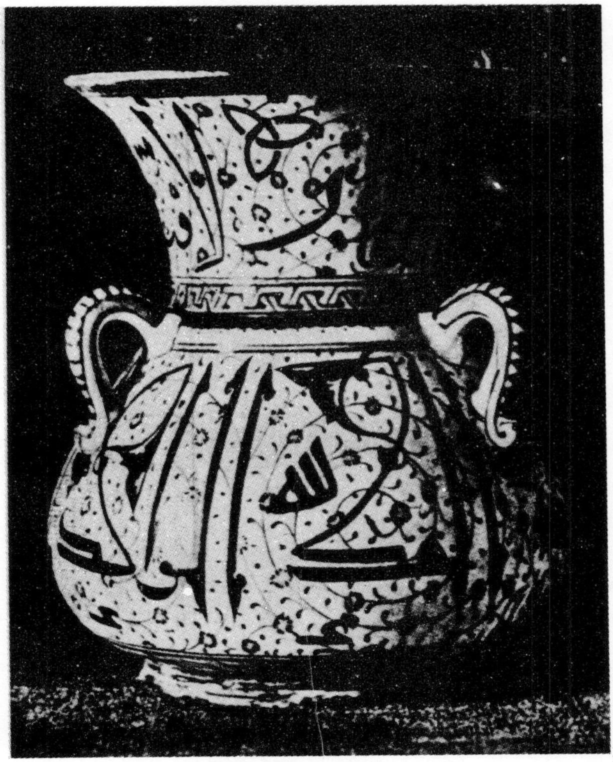

Fig. 112.

A vase with white ground and the inscription painted in blue against a back-ground of light conventional foliage; XVI century, Anatolia.

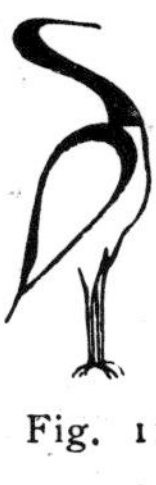

Fig. 113.

How an angle broadens into a curve might be observed by comparing the letter *r* or *d* of the Kufic style with that of the Naskh.[1] In the Kufic these letters are written in the form of an acute angle. In the Naskh this angle broadens into a curve; in the case of *r* into an obtuse curve. The upper arm of the angle is bent at the top towards the right and the lower arm running slantingly towards the left turns upward in a small curve pointed at the top like the sting of a scorpion. If we place this Naskh *r* upside down (fig. 113) its curves would resemble the graceful bends

1. Most of the styles illustrated below are adopted from: Les Calligraphes et Les Miniaturistes, 1908, pp. 21-62; Subhu l-A'sha vol. III, pp. 54-142; Arzhang-i-Cin, 1925 Nazm-i-Parwin, 1935; I'jaz-Raqam 1927; Oriental Penmanship, 1886, etc.

in the long neck of a crane, the base of the letter *r* would suggest the beak of the crane turned towards the right. The curve marking the shoulder of the crane is not used in Naskh, it is peculiar to Nasta'liq, and forms the letter *l* in Nasta'liq placed upside down.

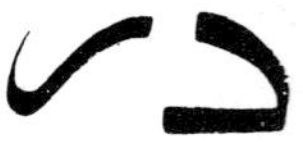

Fig. 114.

The curve forming the base of this letter *r* is peculiar to styles in Naskh (fig. 114). The same curve will be observed in the final flourishes of some other letters of the Arabic script. This curve, which just avoids an angle, becomes a crescent curve in Nasta'liq. Curves and strokes shown in figs. 115—118, are peculiar to Naskh.

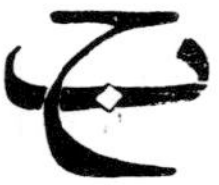

Fig. 115.

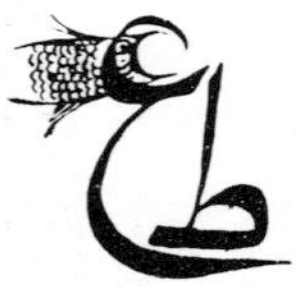

Fig. 116.

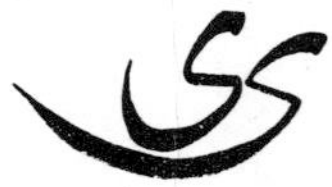

Fig 117.

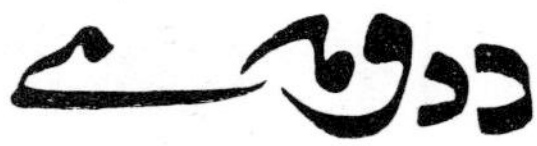

Fig. 118.

Suls is the ornamental variety of the Naskh style. In its structure it differs from the Naskh only in the proportion of its curves

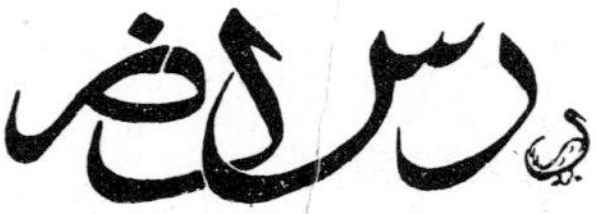

Fig. 119.

and strokes which are about three times the size of the Naskh (fig. 90). The Suls brings out with full emphasis the wavy movement suppressed in the peculiar curves and strokes of the Naskh style. In the Suls style strokes take the form of a dagger and curves run smoothly like waves of water (fig. 88). As this style was generally used as an ornament, architectural or otherwise, it was written in bold curves and

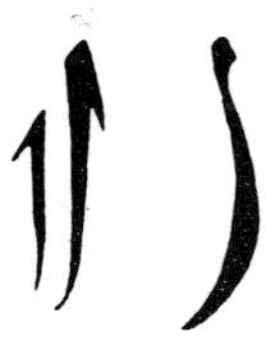

Figs. 120, 121.

wide swinging waves slightly recoiling at their pointed tops. This sweep is common in the Diwani style of the Turks and in Shikasta. The Suls sweep is that of a curved dagger, as shown in figs. 120 and 121. This sweep might be written in Suls in a straight stroke or in a broadly curved one (fig. 122). However, this rebounding stroke is more common to Shikasta than to any other style. The horizontal stroke both straight and curved might be written in Shikasta as shown in fig. 123. Fig. 100 is a beautiful specimen of Shikasta-amiz calligraphy, by Sayed Muhammad Da'ud

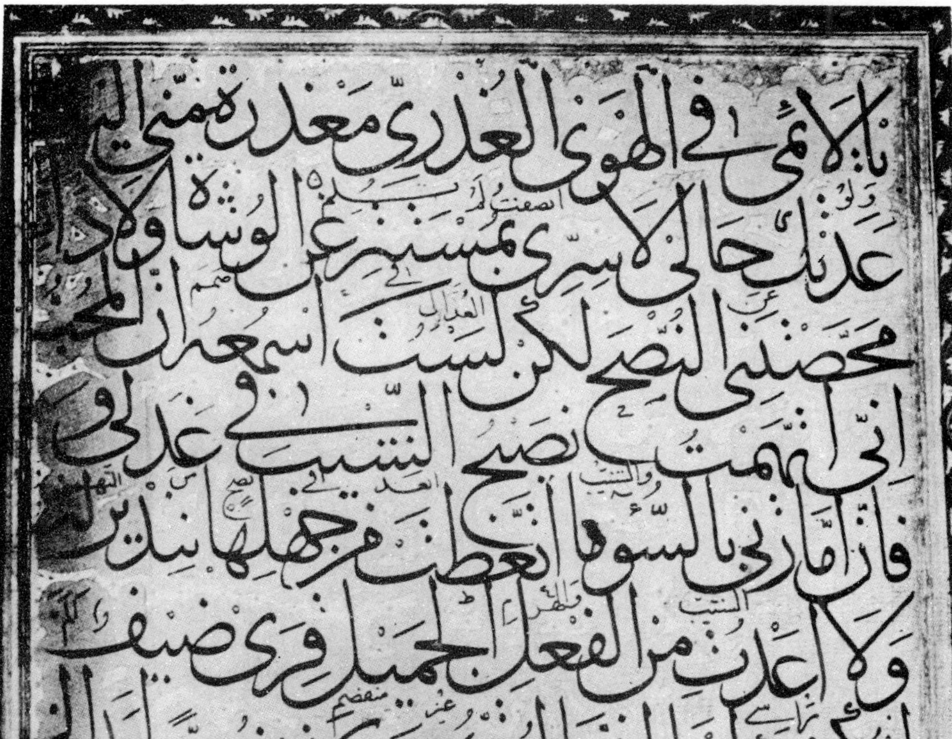

Fig. 122.

A panel in decorative Naskh, written in gold by the celebrated calligraphist 'Abdullah Tabbakh ; Santiniketan Museum.

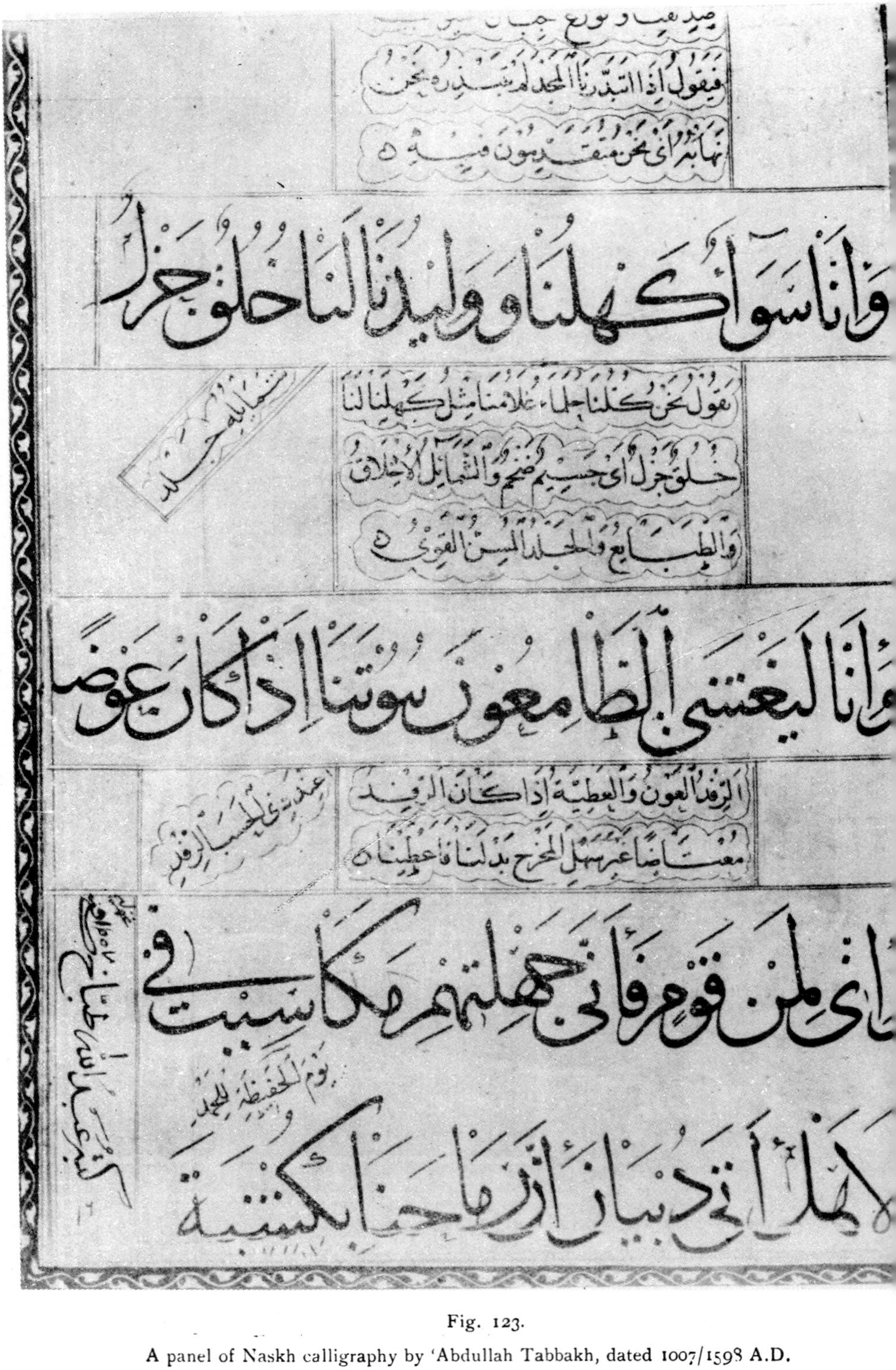

Fig. 123.

A panel of Naskh calligraphy by 'Abdullah Tabbakh, dated 1007/1598 A.D. Santiniketan Museum.

al-Husaini. It is in a style mixed of Nasta-'liq and Shikasta.

Of the ornamental flourishes the most graceful is perhaps that of the style known as Riqa' (fig. 126). It is surely more decorative than Suls. Its strokes move with the grace of a running snake or like the ripples of a stream.

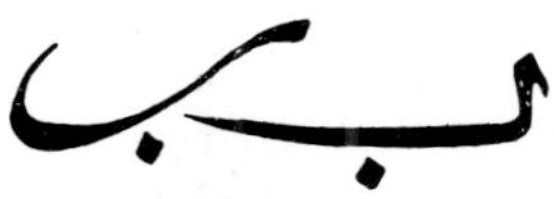

Fig. 124.

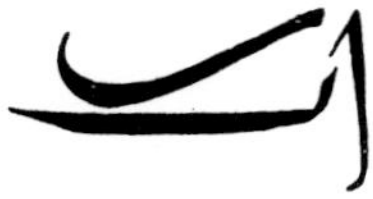

Fig. 125.

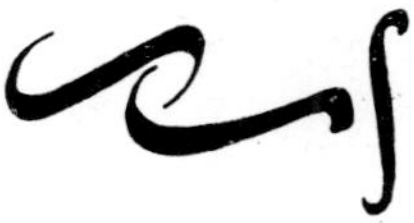

Fig. 126.

Riqa' is not similar to the style known as Tauqi', so far as I can judge. It seems to be only a decorative way of writing the Naskh and resembles Suls. When these curves curl up into small knots and the strokes become more pointed and thinner in their breadth, we have the style called Zulf-i-'arus, i. e. "locks of the bride". It is in fact a decorative style of the Nasta'liq type (figs. 127, 128, 142). Resembling the Suls in its pointed stroke but more peculiar in its execution is the style called Rihan. Its strokes end in straight points and rarely turn up in a curve or a loop, as they do in the Suls and Zulf-i-'arus styles. Its strokes are thick in the middle and gradually become thinner towards their ends. Sometimes they are like straight shafts descending slantingly towards the left. In fact, these strokes are rarely horizontal in their position (fig. 129). In the proportion of its curves and strokes it slightly differs from Suls. The swinging flourishes of the type used in Suls, Riqa' and Shikasta were also used in the old Maghribi Naskh.

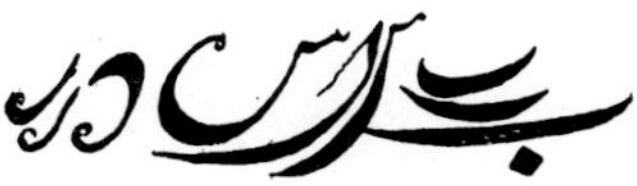

Fig. 127.

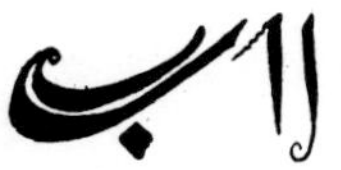

Fig. 128.

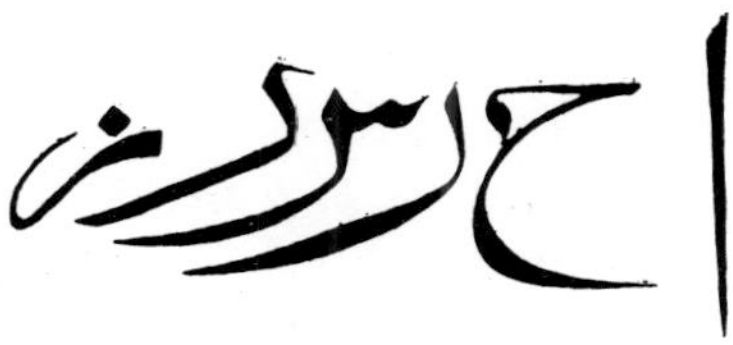

Fig. 129.

The Gulzar and the Ta'us are not styles in themselves, they are purely ornamental treatments of other styles. These are not written with the pen in the regular manner, but are drawn in outline and then filled in with decorative lines (fig. 130), with flowers (fig. 131) or animals like fish or peacock ; in each case the treatment is named differently as Gulzar, Mahi or Ta'us. In Ta'us the letters are traced in a way that they resemble peacocks in their outlines. The spaces within the

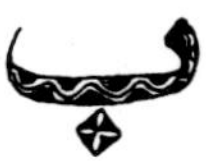

Fig. 130.

outlines of these distorted letters are also decorated with peacock feather drawings.

The Larza too is no independent style by itself. Like the Gulzar and other ornamental treatments it is only a manner of writing any particular style. In the Larza letters are written in a way that they look like 'quivering' twigs. It has no other peculiarity than this that in it the writing appears to have been written by a hand shaking with excitement (fig. 132).

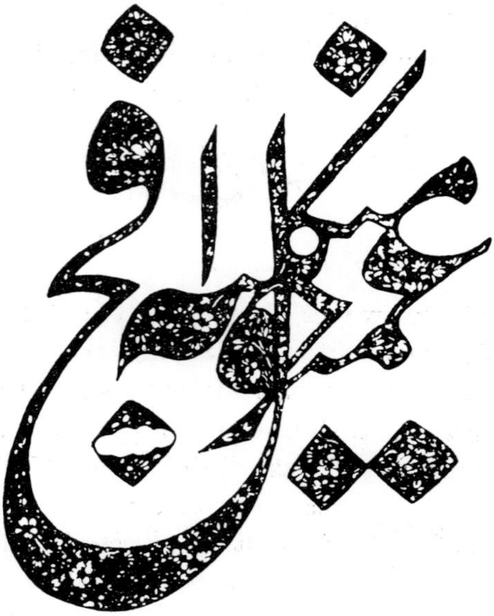

Fig. 131.
A specimen of Nasta'liq treated as Gulzar, by Hamid Husain.

The style called Manshur is a peculiar one. In it letters look exactly like pieces of a tape or ribbon twisted to form letters, with the end of the tape turned round the corners of letters in loops (figs. 133, 134).

Muhaqqiq too is a decorative style. Its strokes break up abruptly and points sometimes project into one or two threadlike fibres, as shown in fig. 135. Like other ornamental styles of calligraphy this one too is used rarely, and only

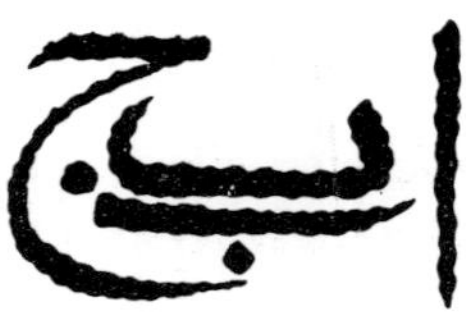

Fig. 132.

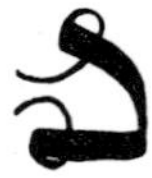

Fig. 133.

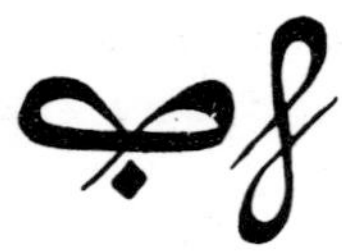

Fig. 134.

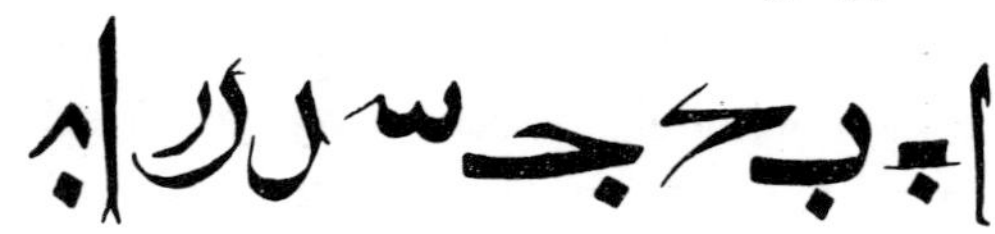

Fig. 135.

as a novelty. This style is written in thick and bold characters. It is similar to Rihan in its proportions of strokes and curves, but is bolder than that in its characters. Another difference which is much more important is that strokes in the Muhaqqiq are seldom written slantingly and none of the horizontal strokes is ever pointed.

Among the decorative styles or decorative treatments of the Arabic script Bihar is perhaps the least decorative. It is a peculiar

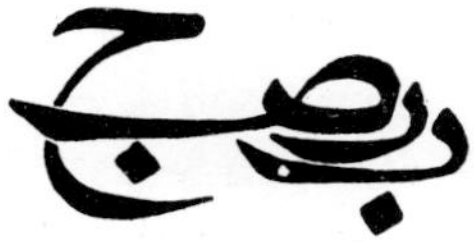

Fig. 136.

style, almost Naskh in the structure of its characters, but its strokes, that shoot horizontally, begin from a thin point and gradually grow thicker towards their left end and either terminate in a sharp point resembling that of Rihan or in a blunt solid point peculiar to the Nasta'liq style (fig. 136).

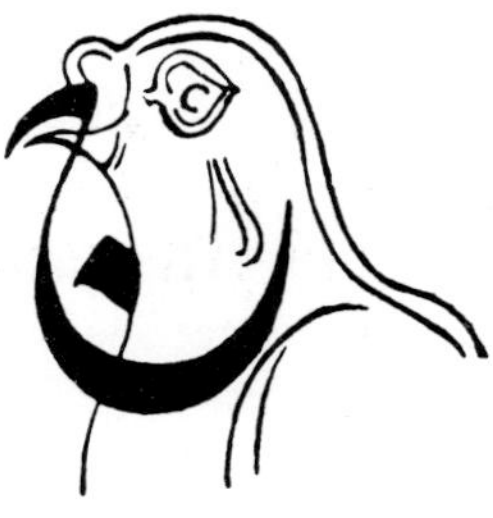

Fig. 137.

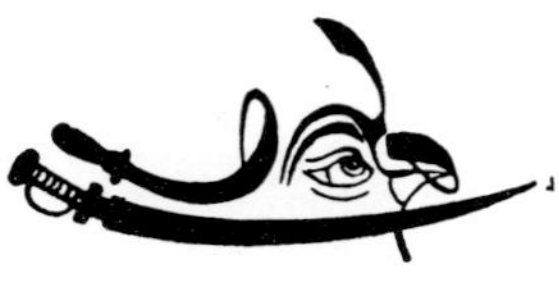

Fig. 138.

The Nasta'liq style is the latest. No other style has succeeded it, nor is it ever likely to be. In it curves develop into most sensual forms—either round and supple like the crescent or smooth and oval like an egg. Its strokes are long and sharply or bluntly pointed in the form of a straight sword or a scimitar. In it strokes flow easily, either straight horizontally, or with a slight gradually increasing bend towards the middle in the manner of a sword. These strokes (excepting those of the letters *k* and *s*) never descend slantingly as they do in Suls, Riqa',Rihan, Diwani and Shikasta (figs. 137-40). The specimen given in fig. 87 might be observed for forming an exact idea of the nature of a Nasta'liq stroke. Curves in the Naskh and Suls are not quite

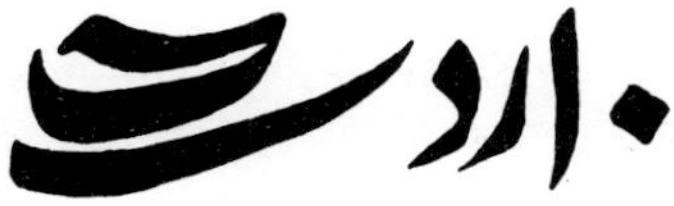

Fig. 139.

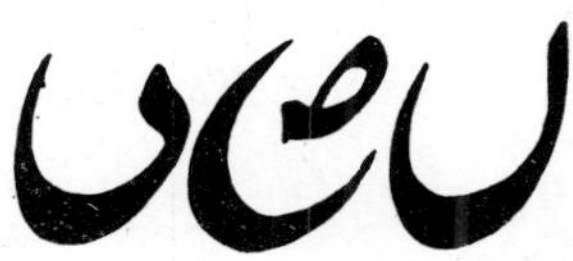

Fig. 140.

round (figs. 122, 123); they have, particularly the Suls ones, the grace of a line that descends down the neck of a duck and passing round the belly ascends to the tip of its tail (fig. 119). This curve is the characteristic curve of the Suls. The wavy character of Suls curves is marked in the curve that is peculiar to letters resembling the letter *j* (fig. 141). This

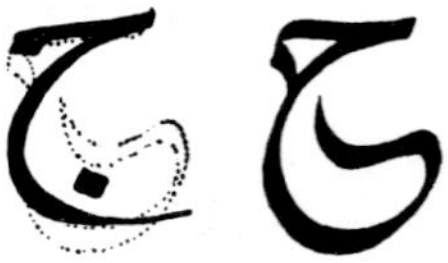

Fig. 141.

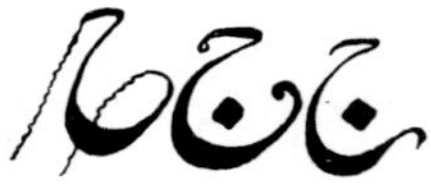

Fig. 142.

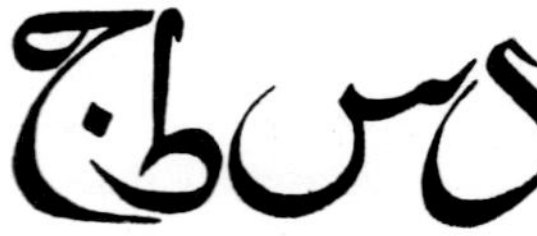

Fig. 143.

curve, but for the recoiling flourish in the centre and at the beginning of the letter, is Nasta'liq in its roundness. Hence not peculiar to the Suls. Other curves like that of the letter *'a* are common to most of the styles (fig. 144). Curves in Zulf-i-'arus, like its strokes, either turn at the end in a coil upward or downward or descend in the form of wavy hair.

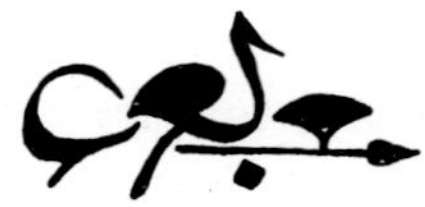

Fig. 144.

Dots or rounded heads of letters like those of the Ar. *m*, *f*, *q*, *w*, or *h* have been written in a variety of ways, some of which are shown in figs. 144 and 145.

There are a few more styles that are mentioned in works on calligraphy, but I have not illustrated them as they are not in any way important as types of writing. For example, the style known as Ghubar is simply a very fine writing. Letters in it are so small that they appear almost as fleeting dust.

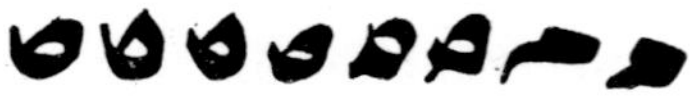

Fig. 145.

The Shafi'a style is derived from Nasta'liq. In this style curves are often left as half curves and prolonged to an extent that they resemble slanting strokes.

The Hilali is a style in which letters are written in a way that they look as if composed of crescent moons.

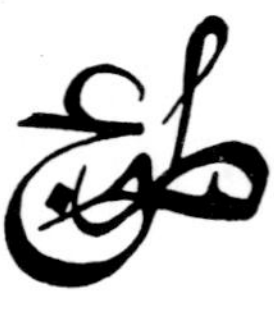

Fig. 146.

The Badral-Kamal, the Vilayat and the Tauqi' (fig. 146) are, properly speaking, imperfect distortions, however ingenious, of the Nasta'liq style.

The Shikasta, or the broken style, is a further simplification of the Nasta'liq, and is, in fact, a sort of short-hand. Letters are rarely disconnected from each other in this commonly used style, nor are diacritical dots or vowels ever written. Though at first sight it looks like having been written in a most careless way, yet it requires much practice and knack. This style came into existence in courts, secretariats and business offices where the writing of letters and other documents had to be done hastily. In it curves turn into long-flung strokes, curved naturally in

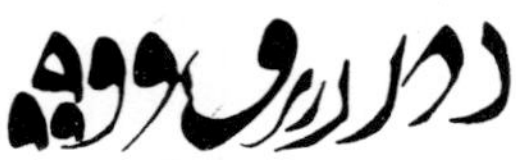

Fig. 147.

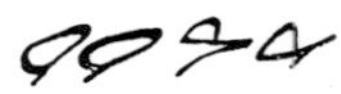

Fig. 148.

the sweep of the pen. Calligraphists have moulded even these broken forms of letters written in haste into some sort of grace. As far as reading is concerned, this style is the most inconvenient (figs. 147, 148).

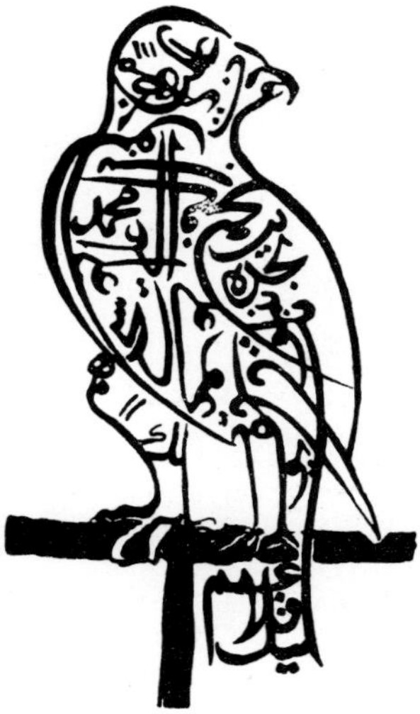

Fig. 149.

The most ingenious use of the Arabic script is the one technically known as Tughra. A sentence from the Koran or a common prayer is written in a way that the composition outlines a bird, or a tiger or an elephant, or any other animal excepting those considered unclean or of ill-omen. Such Tughra writings are used as amulets by the superstitious masses. The lion or the tiger, which are symbolic of the valour of 'Ali, are mostly used in Tughra and the prayer composed of such figures, called Nad-i-'Ali, is addressed to him and is supposed to protect the keepers from the malicious influence of evil spirits.

Such animal figures, in spite of the ban the priest has put on them, form a very common object of decoration used in Moslem homes. They serve the double purpose of decoration and a means of warding off the evil spirit from the house. The figure of the tiger (fig. 151) has a text in Urdu which informs us that a Hindu or Moslem or any one who has faith in this drawing and hangs it on the wall of his house, would be safe from all sorts of evil

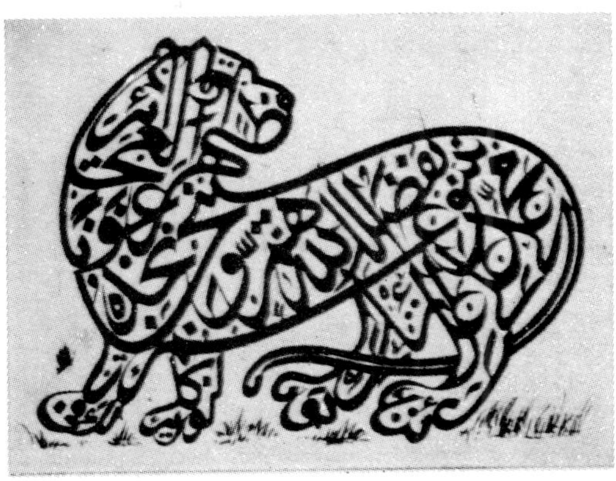

Fig. 150.

influences. The Tughra was written at an auspicious time. A rather favourite form of Tughra used for such magical purpose is the parrot (fig. 149).

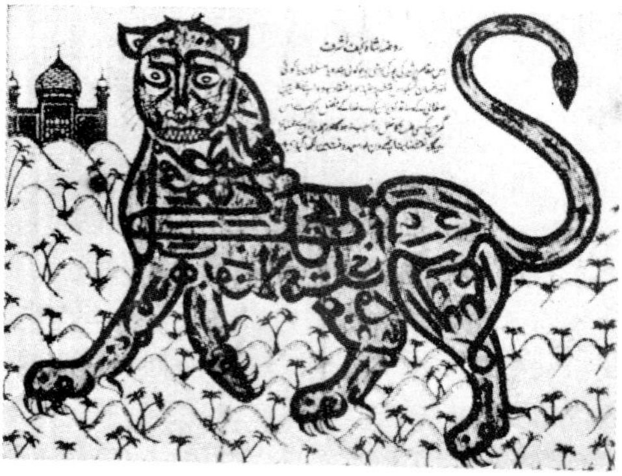

Fig. 151.

Tughra need not be necessarily in animal figures, it might be written in any other ingenious way, as would require a good deal of deciphering before one can read it. Names of Allah, Muhammad, his daughter and those of the succeeding Kalifs are generally written in various becoming ways that help in keeping in mind the characters of those whom the names signify. Fig. 154 shows an example of writing such names in the form of a human head. The elephant, with the *haoda* on its back (fig. 152), is produced by arranging the name and designation of the Nawwab of Tawara.

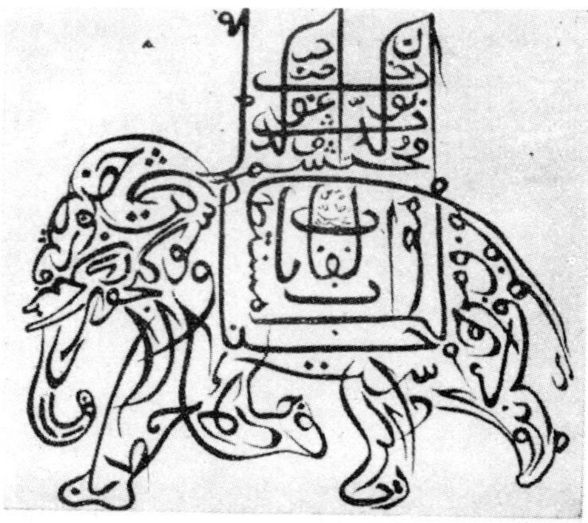

Fig. 152.

I might mention here a very uncommon way of writing in the Tughra style (fig. 153). The writing is done in Kufic and the example belongs to the period when Kufic was not yet obsolete. The upper portion of letters in the writing is so decorated with drawings of human and animal figures that the letters below seem to form part of the lower limbs of their bodies or top shoes worn by them. The decoration is a lively scene of a procession. The letters are shaded deeply to keep in contrast with the figures above them. Tughra is most commonly used in seals, wherein names are engraved in beautiful and fantastic ways (fig. 157). Less like Tughra in decorative form but

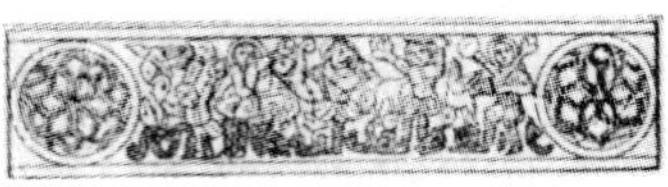

Fig. 153.

more complicated than the ordinary way of writing is the style used in the ornamentation of glazed earthen ware and metal vessels. Like the Kufic, though not in as much complicated manner, Naskh and Nasta'liq styles have been used in the decoration of walls and ceramics (figs. 9, 82, 83, 88, 89, 90, 93, 96, 100, 107, 155-160).

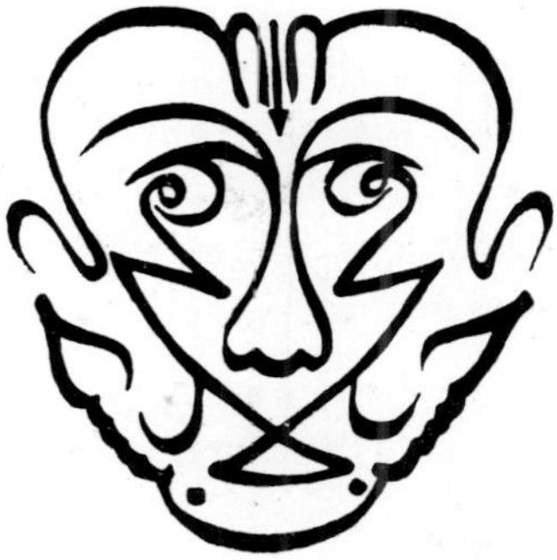

Fig. 154.

The technique and most of the designs used in the decoration of wall sur-

Fig. 155.

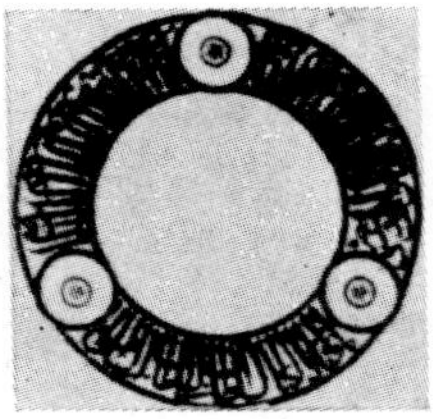

Fig. 156.

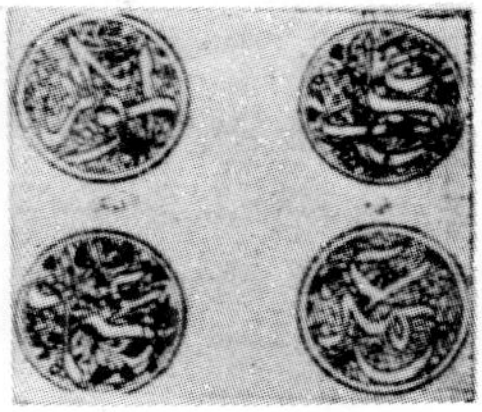

Fig. 157.

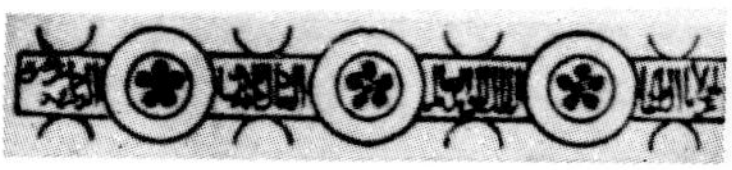

Fig. 158.

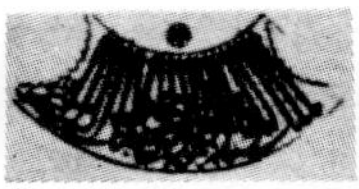

Fig. 159.

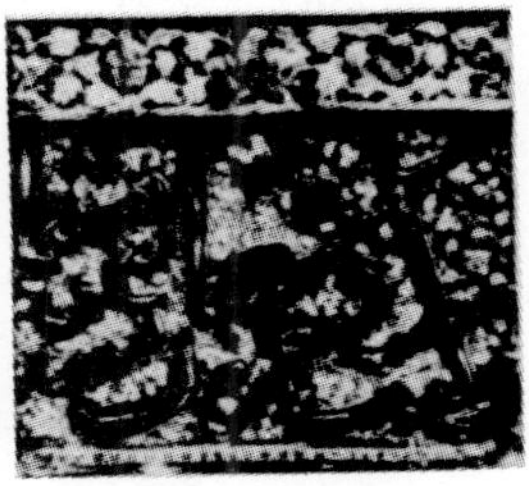

Fig. 160.

faces, and the ceramics were adopted from the Kufic. Particularly the march of perpendicular lines or the concentric convergence of these lines was used in Naskh and Nasta'liq decorations (figs. 82, 83), but the result rarely reached the same fitness of the means with the subject and the perfection that the script decoration had reached in the Kufic period.

The Tughra styles engraved at Murshidabad during the 15th century A. D. (figs. 162, 163) are examples of the type of the decorative style of writing that prevailed in Bengal till the advent of the British. We find that the Kufic model with its verticle strokes running in procession is still before the calligraphist. Excepting in such early architectures as the tomb of Altamash, and the Mosque at Fatehpur Sikri (fig. 9) decorative calligraphy of most of the buildings of the Moslem period is tame in comparison with that of the same period in Persia. Bengal stones perhaps represent the most deteriorated examples of monumental writing. Nothing can be more ugly in writing than the Gour inscription of the reign of Shamsuddin Altamash, dated 633/1235 A. D., inscribed on the well built by Kutlugh Khan. [1] Inscriptions engraved in such atrocious style are common in Bengal. Some of the inscriptions found in Murshidabad district (figs. 162, 163),

Fig. 161.

Detail of an inscription (fig. 93), Mustansir billah's Madrasa (630 A. H.), Baghdad.

are good and perhaps the best among engraved inscriptions found in Bengal. The varticle line is the chief attraction of such inscriptions, while the style of the calligraphy is a mixed one.[2]

Calligraphic painting on silk and ivory and carving on metals, wood, ivory and stone, are, as I have mentioned, among the most

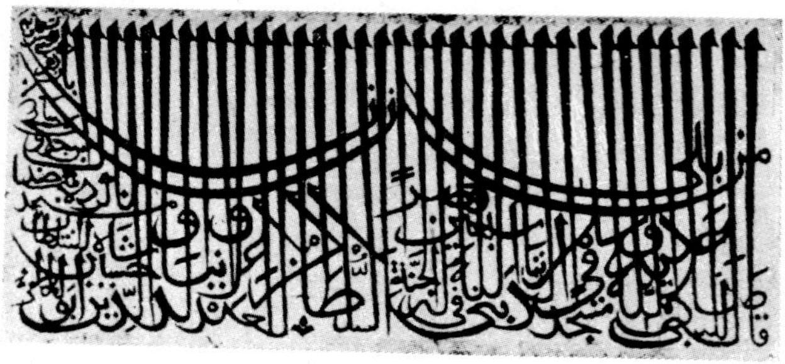

Fig. 162.

Inscription of the reign of 'Ala'uddin Husain Shah, dated 905/1499 A. D., Babargram, Murshidabad.

popular uses of this art. Naskh and Nasta'liq styles, though more difficult of execution on hard material because of their round and

1. Arch. Survey of India, Vol. XV. pl. XX.
2. JASB. N. S. July 1917, plates III, VI.

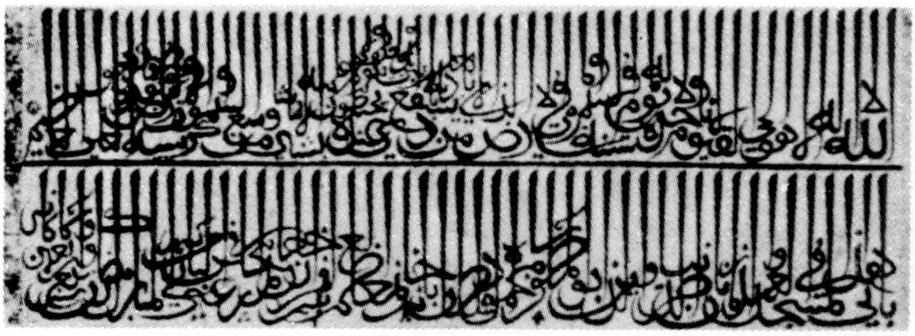

Fig. 163.

Inscription recording the excavation of the tank Sagar Dighi, dated 921/1515, A. D., Murshidabad.

pointed curves and strokes than the angular Kufic, have been used with great success and not infrequently have surpassed the workmanship of the days of the Kufic. The brass tray bearing inscription in decorative Naskh, inlaid with silver, with the name of Sultan Sha'ban[1] (XIV century A. D.), bronze vases and candlesticks, chandeliers, writing cases, Koran boxes and cisterns, etc., inlaid with gold or silver, some of the finest examples of which are preserved in the various museums of Europe, Egypt and Persia, bear calligraphic inscriptions of unapproachable beauty.

BIBLIOGRAPHY.

Huart, *Les Calligraphes et les Miniaturistes de L'orient Musulman*, 1908. De Sacy, *Nouveaux apercus sur l'histoire de l'ecriture chez les Arabes du Hidjaz*, Journal Asiatique. Series I, X, p. 290. Moritz, *Arabic Palæography. Corpus Inscript. Semitic.* part IV. tom. I, 1889, tom. II, 1908, 1911-20. *Epigraphica Indo-Moslemica.* Adolf Grohmann, *Texte Zur Wirtschaftsgeschichte Agyptens in Arabischer Zeit* in the Archiv Orientalni, Oct. 1935, pp. 437-472. Ency. Brit. 14th ed. vol. II. art. Arabia—*Inscriptions*; vol. XVII. art. Persia—*Persian Art* . . . Ency. of Islam, 1913, vol. I. art. *Arabia.* Hughes' Dictionary of Islam, 1885, art. *Writing.* F. Sarre und E. Herzfeld, *Arch. Reise im Euphrat-und Tigris-Gibiet*, 1911, Band I, II, III, IV. F. Sarre, *Die persisch Islamisch Miniaturmalerei*, 1914. Vol. II. E. Blochet, *Les Peintures des Manuscrits Persans de la Collection Martia*, in the Monuments et Memoires 1918-1919. K. A. C. Creswell, *The Great Salients of the Mosque of al-Hakim at Cairo*, in the JRAS. Oct. 1923. S. Flury, *The Kufic Inscriptions of Kisimkazi Mosque, Zanzibar*, 500 H. (A. D. 1107), in the JRAS. Ap. 1922. Lucien Bouvat, *Essai Sur La Civilization Timoride, La Calligraphie* . . ., in the Journal Asiatique, 1926, p. 261. M. N. de Khanikoff, *Les Inscriptions Musalmanes Du Caucase*, in the Journal Asiatique, Aout, 1862. M. C. Ganneau *Notes D'Epigraphie et D'Histoirie Arabes*, in the Journal Asiatique, 1887, p. 472. M.

1. Egyptian Art Through the Ages, p. 316.

Alfred Bel, *Inscriptions Arabes de Fes,* in the Journal Asiatique 1917, pp. 81-, 215-, 304-; 1918, pp. 189-, 337-; 1919, pp 5-. M. Rubens Duval, *Inscriptions Syriaques de Salamas, en Perse,* in the Journal Asiatique. 1885, p. 39-. Belin, *Extrait Du Journal D'un voyage D Peris A Erzeroume,* in the Journal Asiatique. 1825, p. 365-. D. S. Margoliouth, *Early Documents in the Persian Language,* in the JRAS. Oct. 1903, p. 761. F. Krenkow, *Two Ancient Fragments of an Arabic Translation of the New Testament,* in the JRAS. Ap. 1926. *Specimens of Calligraphy in Delhi Museum of Archæology.* No. 29. M. Mahfuzul Haq, *Specimens of Moslem Calligraphy in the Ghosh Collection,* 1927; *Persian painters, illuminators and calligraphists etc. in the 16th century A. D.,* in the JASB. N. S. 1932. p. 239; *Some Specimens of Calligraphy,* in the Rupam, No. 37. Jan. 1929. p. 29. *Four panels of Calligraphy in the Wantage Bequest,* in the Rupam, Jan.—Jun, 1923, p. 34; *Some Mussulman Architectural Ornaments,* p. 39. *Two pages of Mussulman Calligraphy,* in the Rupam, Nos. 22-23, 1925, p. 77. O. C. Gangoli, *A page of Moghul Calligraphy,* in the Rupam No. 30. 1927, p. 59. Burlington Magazine, 1921, 1927, 1928, 1931. Islamic Culture, Oct. 1931, pp. 613, 627; 1932, p. 84, 85. Studio, Jan. 1931, p. 14, Mar. 1931. Kazi A. Akhtar, *The Art of Waraqat during the Abbaside period,* in the Transactions of the 7th A. I. O. Conference, Baroda, 1933. H. Blochmann, *Eight Arabic and Persian inscriptions from Ahmadabad,* in the Indian Antiquary, Oct. 1875, p. 289. Arch. Survey of India: Rajputana, 1882-83; Bengal, 1879-80; Annual Report, 1903-4. G. Migeon *Manual D'Art Musulman,* 1927. T. W. Arnald, *A History of Islamic Painting,* 1928 : *Survivals of Sassanian and Manichaean Art in Persian Painting,* 1924. The Legacy of Islam, 1931. H. Saladin, *Manual D'Art Mussulman,* 1907. M. Blochet, *Musulman Painting,* 1929. F. R. Martin, *The Miniature Painting and Painters of Persia, India and Turkey,* 1912. M. Marteau and H. Vever, *Les Miniatures persanes,* 1913. Upham Pope, *An Introduction to Persian Art,* 1930. Sir. E. Denison Ross, *Persian Art.* Qulqashandi, *Subhu l-A'sha,* Cairo 1914. vol. III. Yaqut, *Irshad* . . . Cairo, 1907. Ibn Khaldun, Tarikh, Cairo, 1284 A. H. Ibn Khallikan, Cairo, 1310 A. H. Ibn Khatib *Nafhut-Tib,* Cairo, 1279. Ghulam Muhammad, *Tazkira-i-Khushnawisan,* 1910. Murqas Samekar Basha, Al-Muthaful-Qibti, Cairo, 1932. parts I. II. *Khatt-u Sawad* and *Majmu'a,* MSS. in the Library of the Asiatic Society of Bengal.

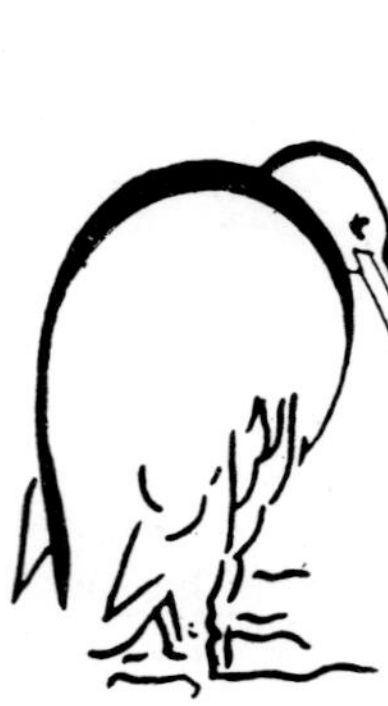